W9-ASG-330

GLEN COVE PUBLIC LIBRARY
GLEN COVE AVENUE
GLEN COVE, NEW YORK 11542

Flowering, Fruiting & Foliage Vines

A Gardener's Guide

Chuck Crandall & Barbara Crandall

Sterling Publishing Co., Inc. New York

ACKNOWLEDGMENTS

Thanks, first for all, to our editor, Hannah Steinmetz, whose dedication, patience, and expert guidance contributed immeasurably to this book. Two others who gave unstintingly of their time answering myriad questions were Kathy Fives of Northwoods Retail Nursery in Canby, Oregon, and horticulturist Vincent Lazaneo.

Designed by Judy Morgan

3 1571 00155 1186

Library of Congress Cataloging-in-Publication Data

Crandall, Chuck.
  Flowering, fruiting & foliage vines : a gardener's guide / by Chuck Crandall and Barbara Crandall.
      p.   cm.
  Includes index.
  ISBN 0-8069-0726-6
  1. Ornamental climbing plants.   2. Ornamental climbing plants—Pictorial works.   I. Crandall, Barbara.   II. Title.   III. Title: Flowering, fruiting, and foliage vines.
  SB427.C727   1995
  635.9′74—dc20
                                                                94-37154
                                                                  CIP

1   3   5   7   9   10   8   6   4   2

Published by Sterling Publishing Company, Inc.
387 Park Avenue South, New York, N.Y. 10016
© 1995 by Chuck Crandall and Barbara Crandall
Distributed in Canada by Sterling Publishing
%, Canadian Manda Group, One Atlantic Avenue, Suite 105
Toronto, Ontario, Canada M6K 3E7
Distributed in Great Britain and Europe by Cassell PLC
Wellington House, 125 Strand, London WC2R 0BB, England
Distributed in Australia by Capricorn Link (Australia) Pty Ltd.
P.O. Box 6651, Baulkham Hills, Business Centre, NSW 2153, Australia
Printed and Bound in China
All rights reserved

Sterling ISBN 0-8069-0726-6

A physician can bury his mistakes, but the architect can only advise his clients to plant vines.
—Frank Lloyd Wright

CONTENTS

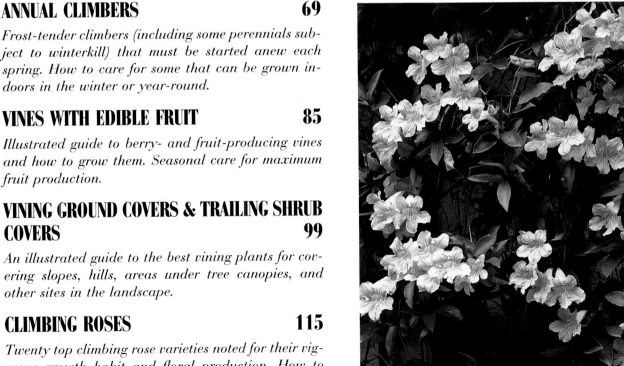

1

Choosing the Right Vine

Wisteria sinensis, Chinese Wisteria

Vining plants have an appealing ability to enhance an entry or front porch with a mantle of beautiful, fragrant flowers; to camouflage unattractive man-made structures, such as chainlink fences and block walls, with a canopy of color or greenery; and to quickly cover steep slopes and "difficult" areas of the yard, like shady spots under trees where nothing else will grow.

You can use vines to screen unsightly views or to give privacy from neighbors, to provide cooling shade, and to afford a continuing source of cut flowers to brighten your interior. In fact, no other plants in nature's vast inventory are more versatile and useful.

You'll find a vine for almost every landscape application. Most are easy-care plants resistant to many of the problems other ornamentals are heir to and can be quickly established and adapted to the need you wish to fill. Nearly all are also easy to propagate.

HOW VINES CLIMB

Many ornamental vines are clingers equipped with holdfasts that help them scamper up a wall. Others have tendrils, and still others are genetically "programmed" to twine around supports to cloak fences, trellises, and columns.

The clingers, like English ivy (*Hedera helix*) and wintercreeper (*Euonymus fortunei*), climb by attach-

Holdfast discs of *Parthenocissus*

ing small rootlets that grow along their stems to surfaces. Other clingers, like Boston ivy (*Parthenocissus tricuspidata*) and Virginia Creeper (*Parthenocissus quinquefolia*), develop branchlets of highly efficient suction cups to pull themselves up walls.

Grape vines (*Vitis* sp.) and sweet peas (*Lathyrus odorata*) use tendrils that wind themselves around wires, cords, and other supports.

Most vines are twiners and climb serpentine fashion, weaving themselves around their support either clockwise (left to right) or counterclockwise (right to left). There is one exception—the tropical loasa. It may decide to grow in either direction.

Among the vines that twine clockwise are kiwi and other members of the *Actinidia* family, *Akebia* species, Dutchman's Pipe (*Aristolochia durior*), American Bittersweet (*Celastrus scandens*), Moonseed (*Menispermum canadense*), Silkvine (*Periploca graeca*), Chinese Wisteria (*Wisteria sinensis*), Scarlet Runner Bean (*Phaseolus multiflorus*), and Morocco Morning Glory (*Convulvulus mauritanicus*).

Some of the species that twine counterclockwise are Chinese Magnolia-vine (*Schisandra chinensis*), Honeysuckle (*Lonicera* sp.), Japanese Hop Vine (*Humulus japonicus*), and Japanese Wisteria (*Wisteria floribunda*).

Most vines twine clockwise, as does the *Actinidia*.

To succeed with vines where you want to grow them, you must familiarize yourself with how they climb and you must provide the appropriate support. Following are all the vining plants commonly used in the garden and classified as clingers, twiners, or tendril climbers.

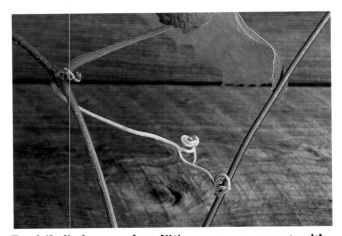

Tendril climbers, such as *Vitis* sp., grasp supports with their tendrils to climb.

CLINGING TYPES

Anemopaegma chamberlaynii/Golden Trumpet Vine*
Campsis grandiflora/Chinese Trumpet Creeper
Campsis radicans/Trumpet Creeper
Decumaria barbara/Climbing Hydrangea
Euonymus fortunei/Wintercreeper
Ficus pumila/Creeping Fig
Hedera helix/English Ivy
Hydrangea anomala/Climbing Hydrangea
Macfadyena unguis-cati/Cat's Claw*
Monstera deliciosa/Split-Leaf Philodendron; Breadfruit
Parthenocissus quinquefolia/Virginia Creeper
Parthenocissus tricuspidata/Boston Ivy, Japanese
    Creeper
Philodendron sp./Philodendrons
Pyrostegia venusta/Flamevine
Schizophragma hydrangeoides/Hydrangea Vine
Scindapsis aureus/Hunter's Robe
*Has claws

TWINING TYPES

Actinidia deliciosa/Kiwi Vine
Actinidia polygama/Silvervine
Adlumia fungosa/Alleghany Vine
Akebia quinata/Five-Leaf Akebia
Allamanda cathartica/Loveflower-of-Guiana
Aristolochia durior/Dutchman's Pipe
Asparagus asparagoides/Gardener's Smilax
Beaumontia grandiflora/Herald's Trumpet
Bougainvillea sp./Paperflower
Calonyction aculeatum/Moonvine, Moonflower
Celastrus orbiculatus/Oriental Bittersweet
Clematis sp./Clematis
Cryptostegia madagascariensis/Rubbervine
Dolichos lignosus/Australian Pea
Gelsemium sempervirens/Carolina Yellow Jessamine
Hardenbergia violacea/Lilac Vine

An entry arbor festooned with jasmine creates an attractive focal point as well as curbside appeal.

Hibbertia scandens/Gold Guinea Vine
Hoya carnosa/Waxplant
Humulus japonicus/Japanese Hop
Humulus lupulus/Common Hop
Ipomoea sp./Morning Glories
Jasminum sp./Jasmine
Lonicera etrusca 'Superba'/Etruscan Honeysuckle
Lonicera japonica 'Halliana'/Hall's Honeysuckle
Lonicera sempervirens/Coral Honeysuckle

Lycianthus rantonnei (Solanum Rantonnettii)/Rantonnett Nightshade

Mandevilla laxa/Chilean Jasmine

Menispermum canadense/Moonseed

Muehlenbeckia complexa/Wirevine

Periploca graeca/Silkvine

Petrea volubilis/Purplewreath

Phaseolus caracalla/Snailvine

Phaseolus multiflorus/Scarlet Runner Bean

Podranea ricasoliana/Ricasol Pandorea

Polygonum aubertii/Fleecevine, Silverlace Vine

Pueraria thungergiana/Kudzu Vine

Quamoclit sp./Starglory

Solanum jasminoides/Potato Vine

Stephanotis floribunda/Madagascar Jasmine

Tecomaria capensis/Cape Honeysuckle

Thunbergia alata/Black-Eyed Susan, Clockvine

Thunbergia grandiflora/Bengal Clockvine

Trachelospermum jasminoides/Confederate, Star Jasmine

Vitis sp./Grape

Wisteria sp./Wisteria

TENDRIL CLIMBING TYPES

Ampelopsis aconitifolia/Monkshood Vine

Ampelopsis arborea/Peppervine

Ampelopsis brevipedunculata maximowiczi/Porcelain Ampelopsis

Anredera cordifolia/Madeira Vine

Antigonon leptopus/Loveline, Coral Vine

Bignonia capreolata/Crossvine

Bryonopsis laciniosa/Bryony

Cardiospermum halicacabum/Heartseed

Cissus capensis/Evergreen Treebine

Cissus incisa/Ivy Treebine

Cissus striata/Striped Treebine

Clematis crispa/Curly Clematis

Clematis montana/Anemone Clematis

Clematis paniculata/Sweet Autumn Clematis

Clematis texensis/Scarlet Clematis

Clematis virginiana/Virgin's Bower

Clytostoma callistegioides/Argentine Trumpet Vine, Violet Trumpet Vine

Cobaea scandens/Purple Bell Cobaea, Cathedral Bells

Distictis cinerea/Trumpet Vine

Exhinocystis lobata/Mock Cucumber

Gloriosa superba/Glory lily

Lathyrus latifolius/Perennial Pea

Lathyrus odoratus/Sweet Pea

Macfadyena unguis-cati/Cat's Claw

Momordica balsamina/Balsam Apple

Pandorea pandorana/Wonga Vine

Parthenocissus heptaphylla/Sevenleaf Creeper

Parthenocissus quinquefolia/Virginia Creeper

Passiflora sp./Passionflower, Passion Fruit

Phaedranthus buccinatorius/Flaming Trumpet

Pyrostegia ignea/Flame Vine

Rhoicissus capensis/Cape Grape

Smilax hispida/Bristly Greenbrier

Vitis aestivalis/Summer Grape

Vitis amurensis/Amur Grape

Vitis argentifolia/Blueleaf Grape

Vitis californica/California Grape

Vitis coignetiae/Gloryvine Grape

Vitis girdiana/Valley Grape

Vitis labrusca/Fox Grape

Vitis vulpina/Frost Grape

SUPPORTS FOR TRAINING VINES

A trellis, arbor, arch, or pergola should be chosen with two criteria in mind: *(1) It should blend architecturally with the style and size of your home, and (2) It should be designed to accommodate the growth habit and scale of the vine(s) you want to establish on it.*

Don't install an ornate, Victorian-style trellis or arbor if your house is a modern ranch or two-storey Spanish design. This would introduce a jarring note into the garden. You can design (or have designed for you) an appropriate support that is more in character with these architectural styles, one that features flat horizontal elements rather than delicate fretwork and curved arches.

Conversely, the classic English-style arbor, pergola, or trellis with latticework and arched top can add a charming touch to cottages, Victorians, and the quintessential American residential design, the craftsman-style home.

Vertical (ladder) lattices of varying heights to match the growth potential of plants are suitable for any house style. Fan-shaped trellises work best against cottage walls and are proportionally in harmony with these single-storey structures.

The second rule to follow in choosing a trellis is to match its structural characteristics with the appearance and bulk of the vine to be grown on it. Light, wispy vines call for lightweight trellises; massive, woody vines require sturdy supports.

To wed the vines to the appropriate support, consider the way the vine climbs and its mature size. For example, twiners must be able to coil around support posts, so vertical elements can't be too broad. Also, most twiners don't require the rugged supports that woody types like grape and wisteria need.

One of the best supports for climbing vines—tendril-bearers and twiners—and those with arching stems (Carolina Yellow Jessamine, jasmines) and

A hinged trellis folds down for wall maintenance.

trailing branches (Ivy geranium, Lantana) is a trellis crafted from rot-resistant wood, metal, PVC, bamboo, or galvanized pipe.

Most large American garden centers and nurseries (and even some lumberyards) carry a variety of ready-made trellises fashioned from cedar, redwood, and pressure-treated lumber, as well as some made from iron, PVC, and aluminum. Several mail-order nurseries also offer a selection of styles. In Canada and Europe hardwoods like oak may be used to make supports and well-crafted wrought-iron versions of clas-

A hinged trellis is hooked overhead with hook-and-eye hardware.

sic styles may be found.

Some U.S. outlets carry attractively designed trellises of pine and other softwoods stapled together and stained a cherry tone to resemble redwood. With these, beauty truly is only skin deep. While they are adequate for supporting lightweight vines, they are not strong enough to carry vigorous woody vines and they won't survive the rigors of exposure to rain and snow for many seasons.

The ready-to-install versions crafted from rot-resistant wood, however, will last indefinitely. The downside is that they are usually a bit pricey. You may find it is more economical to build your own supports, especially if you need several, if you are handy with tools or have a friend who is. Most building supply centers stock rot-resistant lumber in dimensions of 2 x 2″ and 3 x 3″ and lengths from 6′ up to 14′. Stock of thinner dimensions usually must be ripped from broader lumber. Some lumberyards will do this for you, most won't.

Purchasing Lumber

Structural lumber comes from both types of trees—hardwoods, which are broadleaf deciduous species (hickory, oak), and softwoods, which are evergreen conifers (cedar, cypress, redwood). Because of their rot-resistant characteristics and easy availability (except for redwood) and moderate price, softwoods have become the preferred wood for garden construction projects.

In the U.S., lumber-shopping by the inexperienced consumer has been made easier by the creation of a grading system that takes the guesswork out of the process—provided you know what you're looking for. All lumber is stamped with a coded grade that reveals its moisture content, grade, wood type, and other useful data.

Lumber is graded and priced by what part of the tree it comes from, how the grain runs (vertically or flat), how it is finished (rough or surfaced), and how it is dried.

First, let's take the source of the lumber. Sapwood grows next to the bark. It is called sapwood because it contains the growth cells and disperses food and water throughout the tree. It is the most porous wood in a tree and, because of this, it easily absorbs preservatives and stains and—if untreated and sunk in the ground—wicks water from the soil. Its porosity also means that it doesn't hold fasteners as well as heartwood.

Heartwood is from the center of the tree. It isn't as

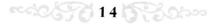

porous as sapwood, and this characteristic helps it resist decay without treatment with additional preservatives. Termites are much less likely to attack heartwood because of its hardness. It yields the most expensive lumber from a tree.

The milling process reveals the grain of the wood. It will have a vertical grain that runs through the length of the board, a flat grain, or both. Vertical-grain lumber is less likely to warp or cup and looks better, so it is most desired. The cost is usually higher for vertical-grain stock.

Lumber is offered either rough or surfaced. Rough means what it says: the surface has not been planed smooth. It may have knotholes, checks, or other defects. Surfaced lumber means the stock has been smoothed and is virtually free of knotholes and other problems.

How the lumber was dried is another important factor. Lumber always contains moisture. The more moisture it has, the less stable it is from the standpoint of shrinkage, checking, warping, or cupping. Green lumber, labeled S-GRN, is unseasoned and contains considerable moisture. Today, only smaller lumberyards stock green wood.

Drying is accomplished either by stacking lumber and allowing it to season in an area protected from the weather or by quick-drying it for a few days in a kiln. There are three grades of seasoned wood—S-DRY, MC 15 (both air dried), and KD (kiln-dried), the preferred grade and the most expensive.

Finally, the cosmetic appearance of wood is also rated. Number 1 is the top grade and signifies the lumber is free of surface imperfections. Number 2 indicates the presence of some tight knotholes. Number 3 may have many knotholes, a few of which may be loose, as well as other blemishes.

Many times, a lower grade of lumber can be used for portions of a project that won't be exposed to view. Save the premium grade for benches and other elements not covered with vines.

In many areas of the U.S., particularly the South, garden structures are crafted from wood (usually southern pine) that has been impregnated with a chemical preservative that is forced into the wood fibres under great pressure. The product is called pressure-treated lumber. It is an economical substitute for the more expensive softwoods like cedar and redwood but can't even come close to duplicating the natural beauty of these two woods.

Treated lumber is not without problems. First among these is a potential health risk if precautions are not taken while handling it. Most treated lumber contains chromium, which is a toxic metal if inhaled. When sawing and shaping treated wood, wear safety goggles, gloves, and a respirator. Scraps should be discarded, not burned, because of the danger of noxious fumes burning produces.

Another problem with pressure-treated wood is that it often contains slits where the preservative was injected. Finally, it frequently has a green tinge that may be objectionable. Two coats of sealer-stain or paint will usually cover both of these cosmetic flaws.

You can treat wood with a preservative and save a bit over purchasing lumber already treated. Although arsenic compounds, creosote, and pentachlorophenol—once widely used preservatives—have been banned for consumer use because of potential health hazards, you can use copper naphthenate, which is environmentally safe. Even so, wear rubber gloves when handling it. It can be brushed on, or posts may be set in a bucket of the chemical for a few hours. Hand-applied preservatives don't penetrate deeply into the wood's interior, but this procedure provides some protection.

Constructing Vine Supports

Trellises and other supports should be assembled with non-rusting galvanized or zinc-coated fasteners; and bear in mind that screws hold better than nails. Supports put together with screws are also much easier to dismantle without damaging the wood, if this ever becomes necessary.

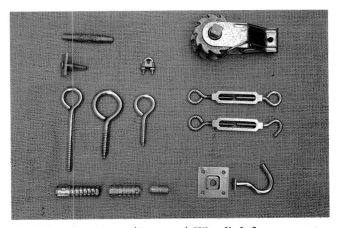

Trellising hardware: (Top row) Wire link for connecting wires; in-line tightener for tensioning wires. (Second row) Wire vise; wire clamp. (Third row) Eye hooks; turnbuckles. (Bottom row) Expanding lag shields; post hook for attaching cable, wire.

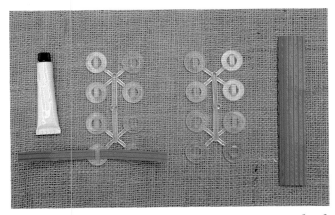

Wall-mounted vine supports: These supports are glued on walls and threaded with twist-ties to hold lightweight vines.

If you are building trellises or arbors for vigorous vines like wisteria, design them to withstand the stresses these heavyweights exert on supports. It is better to start with a structure that seems overdesigned for the skimpy-looking vine you're starting than to find after a few years that the flimsy support that looked more than adequate initially has been wrenched and stressed apart by rampant growth or collapses one day during a windstorm or under the weight of the vine.

One of the most popular, useful, and attractive supports for lightweight-to-medium vining plants is latticework, either diamond- or square-patterned, usually made of cedar in the eastern U.S. and redwood in the west. Panels measuring 4′ × 8′ and smaller are stocked by many larger lumberyards and garden centers. Lattice often serves double duty as handsome fencing material, providing a barrier and some measure of privacy, yet allowing good air circulation. It can be made on site with strips of lath, but this is a time-consuming process. Unless you have a lot of spare time and energy, you may want to call in a professional carpenter to fabricate the panels you need, or check local sources for ready-made latticework.

Ready-made 4′ × 8′ panels of ⅛″ thick lattice retail for about $10; ¼″ thick panels run from $16–$20; panels of ½″ thick lattice cost anywhere from $20–$25, depending on the outlet. Lattice of other thicknesses may be available. Lattice ⅛″ thick splits easily and must be handled carefully. Use it only for lightweight vines. Ready-made supports and construction plans can be found at many large building supply houses.

If you want to tint the wood a specific color (to match the color of your house, for example), use a good-quality sealer and a penetrating stain rather than paint. Paint eventually flakes and deteriorates under the onslaught of sun and harsh weather. Once you have a vine trained on a painted trellis, it is almost impossible to remove it without breaking stems or to paint neatly around it. Stains, however, usually last for the life of the wood (although the color may fade a bit), making stained finishes virtually maintenance-free.

With today's computer color matching, even the most subtle or uncommon color can be duplicated, provided you furnish the mixer a swatch of the color you want. The formula is printed on a sticker affixed to the can, so you are assured successive cans of paint or stain will blend exactly, except for the normal fading that occurs when finishes are exposed to sunlight and airborne contaminants.

Both redwood and cedar may be left natural, treated only with a clear sealer or preservative, stained, or painted. Untreated redwood and cedar age to a greyish-brown many people find appealing. While both redwood and cedar are rot-resistant, moisture can seep in and cause some splitting once their surfaces are penetrated with nails or screws. This usually doesn't undermine their stability, but it does detract from their appearance. Covering fastener holes with a sealer and stain helps to seal these breaches against moisture.

Latticework is difficult to paint or stain with a brush or roller. The best method is to use a spray gun. Panels may be laid across sawhorses or leaned against a wall and sprayed, of course with a protective drop cloth underneath. Because layers that are applied with a spray gun are thinner than those applied with a brush or roller, two coatings are recommended.

Installing Vine Supports

Wooden arches, trellises, and other supports are usually designed so their posts can be sunk into the ground below the freeze line. Eighteen inches is the typical depth for lightweight supports, 24"–30" for heavy-duty types. Lighter supports may be sunk directly into the ground, but large structures that will be carrying the weight of a woody vine, gate, seat, or swing should be embedded in concrete for maximum stability.

Before posts are inserted in the ground, the portion that will be buried should be coated with an oil-base paint or wood preservative to discourage borer insects and prevent rot. Another time-tested method for minimizing insect and rot damage is charring the buried portions of post. For a more stable anchor, 50d or 60d common nails can be driven into the part that will be encased in concrete on all sides.

A posthole digger (sometimes called a clamshell digger) or auger should be used to make the postholes.

These dig a hole only a few inches wider than the diameter of the post, giving the support greater stability than a wider hole dug with a shovel and refilled with tamped backfill.

Traditional lore calls for a stone or a couple of inches of pea gravel in the bottom of the hole before inserting the verticals. This keeps the base of the post off the ground and, theoretically, discourages borers and rot. If the lower section of the vertical has been treated with a preservative, this is unnecessary.

Vertical supports for trellises and arbors must be plumb. Check on two sides with a carpenter's level.

When setting posts into the ground, it is important that they be plumb or the finished structure will lean to one side. Don't trust your eye to make this assessment. Use a carpenter's level to check on two sides. Once the posts are plumb, you should nail braces to them on opposing sides and anchor the other ends of the braces either into the ground or to stakes (see illustration). Use just one nail so the brace can be adjusted.

After installing braces, pour in concrete or pack

Wooden blocks may be used behind wall-mounted vine supports to provide air circulation.

Braces, nailed to vertical supports and attached to stakes driven in the ground, will keep vertical elements plumb while concrete is curing.

backfill soil into the hole with a piece of scrap wood to set the post firmly in place. Check a final time to ensure that the posts are plumb. Adjustments may be made by releasing the bottom end of the brace, leaning gently on the post while watching the bubble in the carpenter's level, then resecuring the brace when plumb has been achieved. Posts set in concrete can be adjusted for up to 20 minutes after installation.

An option to burying posts in the ground is using concrete piers. These are made either with a block of wood embedded in the top for affixing framing anchors or other fasteners or with a metal post anchor already embedded in the top. Piers are typically sunk into the ground onto a footing of concrete with their tops or post anchors at ground level. Make your own piers by digging a hole the appropriate size, pouring in concrete, and installing post anchors before the concrete sets up. Piers and the related hardware needed for these projects are available at larger building supply outlets.

TRELLISES Vertical supports for growing vines against the house should be positioned four to six inches from the wall surface. This provides good air circulation between the plant and the wall and discourages errant stems from invading windows or growing under clapboards or breaches in the surface where wood elements meet brick or stone. Wisteria is notorious for lifting clapboards or shingles if grown directly on a wall.

Spacer blocks of wood may be inserted at intervals behind the trellis to maintain this space. When the blocks are also attached to the wall, they help stabilize trellises against the weight of heavy vines or the destructive effects of severe windstorms. A crossbar of appropriate size should be used to secure the tops of trellises under the eaves. Mending plates are also suitable. They are galvanized metal strips with a hole in each end and are available in a wide variety of sizes.

On wall surfaces that need periodic maintenance and where flexible vines will be trained, you can install wooden trellises that are hinged at the bottom and secured at the top with hook-and-eye latches so they can be tilted away from the wall.

CABLES AND WIRE For sturdiness and permanence nothing surpasses a gridwork of heavy-gauge zinc-coated steel and galvanized wire or vinyl-covered steel cable mounted on the wall. These supports can handle the weight of the heaviest vine, although, occasionally, a wire may need retensioning. Other than this, wire and cable supports are virtually maintenance-free and are nearly invisible when cov-

An arched trellis makes a charming accent against a garden wall.

ered with a mantle of greenery.

These supports are attached to walls by threading them through heavy-duty eye hooks, vine eyes, and other devices embedded in walls. On masonry and stone walls, lag-shields, or expanders, are inserted into holes drilled in the mortar (rather than into the brick or stone) so holes may be neatly repaired if the supports are removed. Eye hooks, vine eyes, or lag bolts are screwed into the lag-shields, which expand to fill the cavity and hold the hook securely in place.

Wires and cables may be fitted with tensioning bolts

or turnbuckles that allow you to tighten or loosen wires by turning the bolt. If a wire should break, or to join the ends of two lengths of wire neatly, devices called wire links enable you to connect wire up to 14 gauge neatly without braiding or crimping ends together. Other devices tension wire and secure the ends of wire runs without twisting or tying (see illustration).

MISCELLANEOUS ANCHORS   For lightweight to medium-weight non-woody vines, affix anchors and tie-offs to walls with strong, waterproof adhesives or embed anchors in brick, stone, or stucco (see illustration). These are suitable for training such climbers as clematis, honeysuckle, jasmine, and some rose varieties.

The following chapter explains how to train vines on various supports and how to use vines in the garden and landscape to get the maximum benefit from each type.

Trellises are excellent supports for vine crops, such as grapes and kiwifruit.

CHOOSING THE RIGHT VINE

2

How to Use Vines

An outbuilding (garden tool storage) soon to be covered with vines.

Many vines are fast growers. Some can cover a post, fence, or arbor in a single season. Annual vines, especially, grow vigorously and are ideal for creating temporary color accents for the summer garden.

For permanence, choose perennial types. In cold-winter areas of the U.S. (Zones 3–8), many perennial vines are pruned back severely or die back with the first hard freeze but rebound in early spring and often grow more vigorously than the previous season. Evergreen vines acclimated to northern climes usually are not seriously damaged by seasonal freezes but go into dormancy until the weather moderates.

Evergreens grown in cold-winter regions do occasionally sustain what is called "foliage burn," a condition that occurs when bitter winds draw the moisture out of leaves. Because the ground is frozen, sap can't rise to replace this moisture and the foliage deteriorates. One way to minimize the chances of foliage burn damaging evergreens is to confine them to walls and other locations away from the brunt of prevailing winds or where hedges and structures provide a protective windbreak.

Frost-tender vines grown in hard-winter areas may be grown in large containers that can be plunged in the ground for the summer, then moved indoors or to a greenhouse until spring. Another method is to wait until frost kills the top growth, then mulch over the crown with a thick layer of insulating mulch. Some gardeners shorten stems, strip the foliage, and cut the roots on one side by slicing through them with a spade. This allows them to tilt the plant over into a prepared trench 12″–18″ deep. A layer of mulch several inches thick is laid over the entire plant and its length is marked at opposing ends by stakes driven into the ground so vehicles and equipment won't accidentally be driven over it.

In frost-free semitropical regions of the U.S. and Sunbelt areas of the South and West, where hard freezes are rare, tender and hardy vines grow year-round, although their rate of growth is slowed considerably by the shorter days and cooler weather of winter. Gardeners in these mild-weather regions are on a different timetable from those in colder climates. Since there is little danger of winterkill of tender growth, vines and other plants are routinely planted in the fall or late winter when other areas are still blanketed with snow and buffeted by severe storms.

When choosing a vine for a specific application, gardeners are sometimes swayed by the appearance of a particular candidate's floral color or leaf shape and decide to make their choice fit the location. This can lead to problems. Weigh several characteristics before making a final decision: How dense is the mature foliage mass? What is the plant's maximum height (or length)? Is it hardy or tender, evergreen or deciduous? Is it a sun-lover or does it need partial shade? Does it bloom, and if so, for how long and what color are the flowers? What method does it use to climb?

If, for example, your goal is to achieve a permanent sight screen for privacy from neighbors and passersby,

***Parthenocissus tricuspidata*, Boston Ivy**

Bougainvillea

you will want an evergreen vine or you've defeated your purpose. A secondary consideration should be rapid growth. Some vines, like Wintercreeper (*Euonymus fortunei radicans*), take years to reach 10 feet while others, such as Boston Ivy (*Parthenocissus tricuspidata*), achieve that height in one season. (See the list of rapid climbers at the end of this chapter.)

Don't limit yourself to just one vine for a specific application. By using two or even three you can achieve interesting effects in foliage textures and shapes and, with flowering types, you can choose species that bloom at different times so that as one is finishing its floral cycle another is just beginning to bud.

Here are some of the uses of vining plants in the garden and landscape.

On Arches, Arbors, and Pergolas

Arches signify a portal into the garden or a garden "room" and are also often used to frame or focus attention on a specific feature beyond, such as a bench, sculpture, or fountain.

Arbors are generally destination points in the garden and often shelter a bench, swing, or retreat for outdoor dining. They usually have walls and roofs of openwork that provide both a framework for vining plants to weave their magic and access for breezes and dappled sunlight to pass through.

It is important not to overpower arches and arbors with vines that are too bold or engulf them so the design is buried under foliage. For arches and delicate-looking arbors with lots of intricate detail, choose plants that are well-mannered and—if a flowering species—ones that bear smaller blossoms.

In both cases, diligent selective pruning to thin and head back vines can open up the greenery to reveal

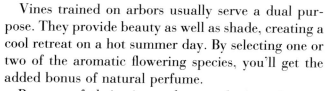

interesting structural forms in the arch or arbor support.

Originally designed to shade garden walks and other large spaces, pergolas differ from arbors in that—unlike most arbors—they have flat roofs, often supported by columns or posts, and are long and narrow with open sides.

Typical plants to festoon arches are delicate flowering species such as Morning Glory and Lady Banks' Rose (*Rosa banksiae*).

Vines trained on arbors usually serve a dual purpose. They provide beauty as well as shade, creating a cool retreat on a hot summer day. By selecting one or two of the aromatic flowering species, you'll get the added bonus of natural perfume.

Because of their size and strength, pergolas can carry the weight and mass of larger vines and vinelike shrubs: Bougainvillea, grape, Joseph's Coat rose, and Wisteria are ideal for displaying more than one vine species.

An entry arch is enhanced with a climber.

A shady garden retreat created with a vine-covered arbor

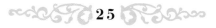

BEST VINE CHOICES

ARCHES

Species	Flowers	Fruit	Zones
Actinidia polygama, Silvervine	x		4–10
Clematis sp., Clematis	x		4–10
Ipomoea sp., Morning Glory	x		5–10
Lonicera sempervirens, Coral Honeysuckle	x		3–9
Mandevilla laxa, Chilean Jasmine	x		10
Menispermum canadense, Moonseed	x		5–9
Passiflora sp., Passionflower	x	x	5–10
Phaseolus caracalla, Snailvine	x		7–10
Phaseolus multiflorus, Scarlet Runner Bean	x	x	4–10
Rosa sp., Climbing Rose	x		5–10
Stephanotis floribunda, Madagascar Jasmine	x		9–10
Thunbergia alata, Black-Eyed Susan Vine	x		4–10
Thunbergia grandiflora, Bengal Clockvine	x		8–10
Vitis sp., Grape		x	6–10

ARBORS

Species	Flowers	Fruit	Zones
Actinidia chinensis, Kiwifruit		x	8–10
Actinidia polygama, Silvervine	x		4–10
Antigonon leptopus, Coralvine	x		8–10
Beaumontia grandiflora, Herald's Trumpet	x		10
Bougainvillea sp., Bougainvillea	x		9–10
Clematis sp., Clematis	x		4–10
Distictis sp., Trumpet Vine	x		9–10
Gelsemimum sempervirens, Carolina Yellow Jessamine	x		7–10
Jasminum sp., Jasmine	x		8–10
Lonicera sp., Honeysuckle	x		4–10
Passiflora sp., Passionflower	x	x	9–10
Polygonum aubertii, Fleecevine, Silverlace Vine	x		5–10
Rosa sp., Climbing Rose	x		5–10
Trachelospermum jasminoides, Star Jasmine	x		7–10
Vitis sp., Grape		x	6–10
Wisteria sp., Wisteria	x		5–10

HOW TO USE VINES

PERGOLAS

Species	Flowers	Fruit	Zones
Actinidia chinensis, Kiwifruit		x	8–10
Aristolochia durior, Dutchman's Pipe			4–10
Beaumontia grandiflora, Herald's Trumpet	x		10
Bougainvillea sp., Bougainvillea	x		9–10
Clematis sp., Clematis	x		4–10
Humulus sp., Hop Vine		x	5–10
Lonicera sempervirens, Trumpet Honeysuckle	x		4–10
Rosa sp., Climbing Roses	x		5–10
Vitis sp., Grape		x	6–10
Wisteria floribunda, Japanese Wisteria	x		4–10
Wisteria sinensis, Chinese Wisteria	x		5–10

On Trellises, Posts, and Columns

By far the most popular supports for training vines in the home landscape are trellises and posts. For the former, twiners and some tendril climbers are most suitable. For the latter, twining climbers are best, provided posts are not too broad for the vine chosen to coil around.

Occasionally, trees are used to grow vines—usually the twining types. While this is a matter of personal taste, trees as vine supports are not the ideal choice, especially if a woody vine species is used. These vigorous vines can constrict the tree as they engulf it and eventually kill it.

Other types of vines grown on trees often weave through the upper branches and become a tangle of growth that is difficult to maintain, creating an oddity in the garden that detracts from the appearance of both the tree and the vine.

Climbing roses trained on trellises.

BEST VINE CHOICES

TRELLISES

Species	Flowers	Fruit	Zones
Actinidia chinensis, Kiwifruit		x	8–10
Actinidia polygama, Silvervine	x		4–10
Akebia quinata, Five-Leaf Akebia			4–9
Aristolochia durior, Dutchman's Pipe			4–10
Celastrus sp., Bittersweet		x	4–9
Clematis sp., Clematis	x		4–10
Gelsemium sempervirens, Carolina Yellow Jessamine	x		7–10
Lonicera sp., Honeysuckle	x		4–10
Mandevilla laxa, Chilean Jasmine	x		10
Rosa sp., Climbing Roses	x		5–10
Trachelospermum sp., Confederate, Star Jasmine	x		7–10
Wisteria sp., Wisteria	x		5–10

POSTS, COLUMNS

Species	Flowers	Fruit	Zones
Beaumontia grandiflora, Herald's Trumpet	x		10
Clematis sp., Clematis	x		4–10
Hibbertia scandens, Gold Guinea Vine	x		10
Ipomoea sp., Morning Glory	x		4–10
Jasminum sp., Jasmine	x		8–10
Kadsura japonica, Scarlet Kadsura	x		7–9
Lonicera sp., Honeysuckle	x		4–10
Schisandra chinensis, Chinese Magnolia Vine	x		4–9
Wisteria sp., Wisteria	x		4–10

On Houses and Chimneys

The right vining plant can soften the hard edges of a structure and add a charming accent, but vines should not obscure the interesting architectural details of a house. Opt for a vine that traces an intriguing pattern on a wall (Creeping Fig), rather than using a rampant, large-foliage vine that will, in time, completely cover a wall (Boston Ivy). Even Creeping Fig will need occasional shearing when it matures to keep it in check.

Clingers are the obvious choice for house walls and chimneys. Clingers such as Boston Ivy have an undeserved reputation for creating rot problems by trapping water against clapboards, shingles, and other wood surfaces. The truth is that their overlapping foliage actually *protects* surfaces by shedding water and helping keep a wall dry. It should be noted, though, that the suction cups and holdfasts of some clingers are difficult to remove cleanly and can bond with wood and damage it by pitting unfinished material or embedding their rootlets into surface finishes. For this reason, clinging types should be restricted to brick, stone, and stucco.

One additional misconception about clinging vines is that they can undermine the mortar between bricks in masonry walls. While this may occur to some extent in older masonry structures where the mortar may already be deteriorating, there is little chance of this problem arising in recently constructed (20th-century) brick walls.

Also be aware that rampant vines like ivy and Wisteria growing over a shingle roof can work their way under shingles and cause leaks. Periodic checking and selective pruning can prevent this.

SOIL PROBLEMS AROUND FOUNDATIONS

To enhance a vine or shrub's chance for a vigorous start, some attention must be given to the soil around the foundation of the house. If this soil has not been improved or replaced to a depth of a foot or more, it may be contaminated with man-made chemicals and

Ficus pumila, **Creeping Fig, is a favorite warm-winter climber for covering walls.**

impurities that can affect the health and vigor of plants grown in it.

Often when homes are built, leftover paint, chemicals, and construction debris are dumped into foundation soil and buried instead of being disposed of in a responsible manner. Ideally, *all* the soil extending three or four feet from the foundation and two feet deep should be replaced, but this is often not practical. In lieu of this, whenever you set in plants at the foundation, dig holes two feet across and deep. Discard this soil and replace it with a mix of equal parts compost, topsoil, and milled (ground) peat moss.

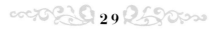

BEST VINE CHOICES

CLIMBERS

Species	Flowers	Fruit	Zones
Anemopaegma chamberlaynii, Golden Trumpet Vine	x		9–10
Beaumontia grandiflora, Herald's Trumpet	x		10
Bougainvillea sp., Bougainvillea	x		9–10
Clematis sp., Clematis	x		4–10
Clytostoma callistegioides, Argentine Trumpet Vine	x		9–10
Distictis sp., Trumpet Vine, Creeper	x		9–10
Jasminum sp., Jasmine	x		8–10
Rosa sp., Climbing Roses	x		5–10
Wisteria sp., Wisteria	x		5–10

CLINGERS

Species	Flowers	Fruit	Zones
Campsis sp., Trumpet Creeper	x		4–10
Euonymus fortunei, Wintercreeper			5–10
Ficus pumila, Creeping Fig			9–10
Hedera helix, English Ivy			5–10
Hydrangea anomala, Climbing Hydrangea	x		5–9
Macfadyena unguis-cati, Cat's-Claw	x		8–10
Parthenocissus quinquefolia 'Engelmanni', Engelmann Creeper			4–10
Parthenocissus tricuspidata, Boston Ivy			4–10

HOW TO USE VINES

Although fashioned from open latticework, this privacy fence performs its function when covered with vines.
Cascading Ivy Geraniums in containers grow merrily along the top.

On Fences, Garden Walls, and Screens

A fence that is not in the best condition, a homely chainlink fence, or a garden wall that needs the softening touch of a mantle of greenery can all be enhanced by training vines on them.

For chainlink, lattice, and other open-weave fences, the ideal vine is a climbing type with tendrils that can help anchor the plant while it wends its way in and out of openings. Rampant annual vines, such as Morning Glory with its many improved cultivars offering a variety of floral color, are well suited to the task of camouflaging a chainlink fence quickly.

Twining vines and vinelike plants are also suitable for training on open-weave fences, but these usually need a little initial guidance. In temperate regions, Bougainvillea is a popular choice for chainlink and wrought-iron fences, but their trailing branches must be tied off periodically to keep them in place. In the eastern U.S. Wisteria is frequently used. It also requires occasional anchoring to its support as well as heading back to keep it in check, but care must be taken not to remove too much leader growth or the vine will not flower.

When training twiners, bear in mind that some twine clockwise and others counterclockwise (see Chapter 1). All that is required is to lead the stem to its support and tuck its tendril behind. It will do the rest.

If your preference is to grow vines over but not *on* fences and walls, or if you want to use climbers on solid surfaces, adapt the same anchor supports described in Chapter 1 and shown in the accompanying photos.

BEST VINE CHOICES

FENCES

Species	Flowers	Fruit	Zones
Aristolochia durior, Dutchman's Pipe			4–10
Bougainvillea sp., Bougainvillea	x		9–10
Campsis grandiflora, Chinese Trumpet Creeper	x		7–8
Campsis radicans, Trumpet Creeper	x		4–8
Celastrus sp., Bittersweet		x	4–9
Clematis sp., Clematis	x		4–10
Hedera helix, English Ivy			5–10
Ipomoea sp., Morning Glory	x		4–10
Lathyrus odoratus, Sweet Pea	x		4–10
Lonicera sp., Honeysuckle	x		4–10
Parthenocissus quinquefolia, Virginia Creeper			4–10
Parthenocissus tricuspidata, Boston Ivy			4–10
Phaseolus caracalla, Snailvine	x		7–10
Rosa sp., Climbing Roses	x		5–10
Thunbergia grandiflora, Bengal Clockvine	x		8–10
Vitis sp., Grape		x	6–10

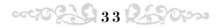

BEST VINE CHOICES

GARDEN WALLS

Species	Flowers	Fruit	Zones
Bougainvillea sp., Bougainvillea	x		9–10
Campsis grandiflora, Chinese Trumpet Creeper	x		7–8
Campsis radicans, Trumpet Creeper	x		4–8
Clematis sp., Clematis	x		4–10
Euonymus fortunei, Wintercreeper			5–10
Ficus pumila, Creeping Fig			9–10
Hedera helix, English Ivy			5–10
Hydrangea anomala, Climbing Hydrangea	x		4–9
Lonicera sp., Honeysuckle	x		4–10
Parthenocissus quinquefolia, Virginia Creeper			4–10
Parthenocissus tricuspidata, Boston Ivy			4–10
Rosa sp., Climbing Roses	x		5–10
Schizophragma hydrangeoides, Japanese Hydrangea Vine	x		5–9

BEST VINE CHOICES

SCREENS

Species	Flowers	Fruit	Zones
Arctostaphylos uva-ursi, Bearberry		x	4–8
Bougainvillea sp., Bougainvillea	x		9–10
Euonymus fortunei 'Argeneo marginata', Silver Edge Wintercreeper			4–8
Euonymus fortunei 'Minima', Baby Wintercreeper			4–8
Euonymus fortunei 'Vegeta', Evergreen Bittersweet			4–8
Gelsemium sempervirens, Carolina Yellow Jessamine	x		7–10
Hedera helix, English Ivy			5–10
Lonicera japonica 'Halliana', Hall's Honeysuckle	x		4–10
Lonicera japonica chinensis, Chinese Honeysuckle	x		4–10
Trachelospermum sp., Star Jasmines	x		7–10

Vine combinations adorn a house wall.

HOW TO USE VINES

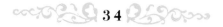

On garden walls the obvious choice is a clinger, such as an evergreen Wintercreeper variety (*Euonymus* sp.) and English Ivy (*Hedera helix*), or deciduous foliage types. For floral displays, roses, honeysuckles, and annual vines provide a long blooming season.

Screens are like free-standing trellises and are used to block unsightly views and achieve privacy in outdoor spaces exposed to public view. But there are other applications, such as using them in front of structures to provide supports for vines and for separating the garden into various "rooms." Normally, screens are small enough to be portable so they can easily be moved to other locations when they are no longer needed in their original site, although they are just as often installed permanently. Temporary screens should not be embedded in concrete, obviously, since this would make their removal difficult.

Latticework screens draped with vines may be used to good effect to "dress up" outbuildings, sheds, carports, and garages. Depending on their configuration, a number of vining and vinelike plants can be grown on screens. Those intended to block views should be covered with an evergreen type or their usefulness will be substantially reduced for nearly half a year.

A vine-covered sight screen provides privacy for a spa beyond.

In Containers and Hanging Baskets

Almost any vining and vinelike plant may be grown in containers, at least for a season or two, but there are a number of species that adapt well to permanent container culture. These—especially flowering varieties—make appealing accents for entries, terraces, decks, and patios.

Growing specimens in pots has some distinct advantages for the avid vine devotee. Primary among these is that gardeners in harsh-winter regions can grow most of the frost-tender tropical and subtropical

***Mandevilla splendens* makes a good container plant.**

Bougainvillea

types and move them indoors or to a greenhouse before the first frost.

Evergreen species may be kept as houseplants until spring then moved outdoors when the weather moderates. Deciduous types may be held in a protected environment in a dormant state until all danger of frosts and freezes has passed.

Another advantage is that vine fanciers who live in apartments, co-ops, or condos, where outdoor ground space is limited or non-existent, can create handsome vertical gardens by growing vines in pots and training them up trellises or other supports anchored in the containers.

An additional benefit is portability. Pots with vines can be moved around to take advantage of sun or shade, as their cultural requirements demand, and to add a splash of color or greenery in a new location.

Containers for vining plants may be made of wood, terra-cotta (clay), ceramic, concrete, metal, or plastic. Sizes should be ample and commodious to provide sufficient room for root development. Vigorous, woody vines are often deep-rooted and will eventually need a large (24″–36″ diameter) container to support their bulk without tipping over, but they may be started in smaller pots, then potted on as they mature.

Half whiskey barrels, rot-resistant wooden boxes, and terra-cotta tubs at least 24″ in diameter are popular choices for growing larger vines (kiwis, roses, wisteria). Smaller vines (Creeping Fig, ivies) don't need this much space for many years. In fact, they seem to prosper in "tight shoes"—containers that restrict their root development—at least for two or three years. Their response is usually to produce abundant foliage and blooms, if flowering types are grown. But check potted vines seasonally to make sure they are not becoming potbound, a condition in which the roots have coiled themselves around each other so tightly they can no longer develop and function normally. This won't kill a plant, but it can stunt its growth and sap its vigor. Guidelines for planting vines in containers can be found in Chapter 9.

A number of vining and trailing plants do well in hanging containers of moss and wire, plastic, terracotta, and other materials. In the absence of garden space, growing plants in suspended containers is often the only option.

Most garden centers stock a variety of containers and devices for hanging them. The most popular are the woven wire types one lines with a layer of damp sphagnum moss that, when dried and formed to the interior walls of the basket, holds the planting mix. In addition to planting in the top, seedlings can be added to the sides by making holes through the moss and inserting plants.

Trailing plants add a charming touch to window boxes and can visually "carry" box gardens when flowering species started with them begin to fade.

A good, lightweight planting medium for containers and hanging baskets is a 50–50 mix of milled (ground) peat moss and compost or potting soil and two cups of vermiculite or perlite. Vermiculite and perlite both help keep the planting mix moist so you won't have to water as often. Vermiculite absorbs water; perlite traps and holds moisture on its surface. When mixing planting media containing peat moss, always soak it thoroughly in warm water to get it wet, then squeeze out most of the water. Peat is extremely difficult to moisten. Once it is damp, never let it dry out completely.

Watch contained garden plants for flagging during

Jasmine planted in raised planters climbs gracefully up a house wall.

hot, windy weather. This indicates dehydration, since the mix in hanging baskets and window boxes tends to dry out more rapidly than soil in a conventional garden. Your goal should be to keep the mix just barely moist. This often means irrigating early in the morning every day through the summer. This chore can be made a breeze if contained gardens are rigged with a drip irrigation system that operates automatically with a preset timer or one that can be turned on manually to water everything at once.

Drip irrigation tubing is quite thin and may be neatly affixed to posts, columns, or walls so it is barely noticed. Complete drip systems containing a variety of emitters (heads) and everything needed to install them are reasonably priced and available at many garden centers and through mail order sources.

Plants grown in baskets and boxes need periodic grooming to stay attractive. Pinch out the ends of trailing and vining plants when they begin to look scraggly, leggy, or grow too long. This will force plants to produce more foliage and flowering types more blooms. Change color seasonally. Once early annuals are spent, uproot them and add summer bloomers to carry the contained gardens into fall.

In addition to seasonal color such as impatiens, pansies, and petunias, some of the many appropriate trailing/vining plants for hanging baskets, containers, and window boxes are listed below.

BEST PLANT CHOICES
CONTAINERS, HANGING BASKETS

Species	Foliage	Flowers	Type
Asparagus scandens, Basket Asparagus	x		Per
Asparagus 'Sprengeri', Sprenger Asparagus	x		Per
Bougainvillea sp., Bougainvillea		x	T. Shrub
Cissus sp., Ivies	x		Ev. Vine
Fuchsia procumbens, Fuchsia		x	T. Shrub
Lantana sp., Lantana		x	T. Shrub
Mandevilla laxa, Chilean Jasmine		x	T. Vine
Pelargonium peltatum, Ivy Geranium		x	Per
Plumbago auriculata, Cape Plumbago		x	S-Ev. Vine
Rosa sp., Climbing Roses		x	H. Shrub
Rosmarinus officinalis 'Prostratus', Trailing Rosemary	x		H. Shrub
Thunbergia alata, Black-Eyed Susan		x	P. Vine
Tropaeolum majus, Trailing Nasturtium		x	Per
Vinca major, Big Periwinkle	x		Ev. Per

EV = Evergreen   H = Hardy   P/Per = Perennial   S-Ev = Semi-Evergreen   T = Tender

HOW TO USE VINES

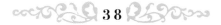

Climbing roses and
Bougainvillea

***Ficus pumila*, Creeping Fig**

FAST-GROWING VINES

Actinidia sp.	Kiwi
Antigonon leptopus	Coral Vine
Aristolochia durior	Dutchman's Pipe
Beaumontia grandiflora	Herald's Trumpet
Bougainvillea sp.	Bougainvillea
Calonyction aculeatum (Ipomoea alba)	Moonflower
Campsis sp.	Trumpet Creeper
Celastrus sp.	Bittersweet
Clytostoma callistegioides	Violet Trumpet Vine
Cobaea scandens	Coral Bells
Distictis sp.	Trumpet Vine
Ficus pumila	Creeping Fig
Hedera helix	English Ivy
Humulus sp.	Hop Vine
Hydrangea anomala	Climbing Hydrangea
Ipomoea sp.	Morning Glories
Jasminum polyanthum	Chinese Jasmine
Lonicera sp.	Honeysuckles
Parthenocissus sp.	Boston Ivy, Virginia Creeper
Passiflora sp.	Passionflower, Passionfruit
Polygonum aubertii	Silverlace Vine
Rosa sp.	Roses
Solandra maxima	Cup of Gold Vine
Trachelospermum sp.	Confederate Jasmine, Star Jasmine
Tropaeolum sp.	Nasturtium
Vitis sp.	Grape
Wisteria sp.	Chinese Wisteria, Japanese Wisteria

SHADE-TOLERANT VINES

Actinidia polygama	Silvervine
Akebia quinata	Five-Leaf Akebia
Aristolochia durior	Dutchman's Pipe
Clematis sp.	Clematis
Euonymus sp.	Euonymus

Ficus pumila	Creeping Fig
Gelsemium sempervirens	Carolina Yellow Jessamine
Hardenbergia sp.	Lilac Vine
Hedera sp.	Ivies
Hydrangea anomala	Climbing Hydrangea
Lonicera sp.	Honeysuckles
Menispermum canadense	Moonseed
Parthenocissus sp.	Boston Ivy, Virginia Creeper
Smilax hispida	Bristly Greenbrier
Thunbergia gibsonii	Orange Clockvine
Trachelospermum jasminoides	Confederate, Star Jasmine
Vitis sp.	Grapes

Clematis sp.

VINES WITH FRAGRANT FLOWERS

Actinidia deliciosa	Kiwi
Anredera cordifolia	Madeira Vine
Beaumontia grandiflora	Herald's Trumpet
Calonyction aculeatum (Ipomoea alba)	Moonflower
Clematis armandii	Evergreen Clematis
Dioscorea batatas	Cinnamon Vine
Distictis laxiflora	Vanilla Trumpet Vine
Gelsemium sempervirens	Carolina Yellow Jessamine
Jasminum sp.	Jasmine
Lathyrus odoratus	Sweet Pea
Lonicera sp.	Honeysuckles
Mandevilla laxa	Chilean Jasmine
Rosa sp.	Roses
Stephanotis floribunda	Madagascar Jasmine
Trachelospermum jasminoides	Confederate, Star Jasmine
Wisteria sp.	Wisteria

Actinidia deliciosa, Kiwifruit

HOW TO USE VINES

Stephanotis floribunda,
Madagascar Jasmine

Clematis 'Henryi'

VINES BY FLOWER COLOR

White (Tender)

Antigonon leptopus alba	Chain-of-Love
Beaumontia grandiflora	Herald's Trumpet
Clerodendron thompsoniae	Tropical Bleeding Heart
Jasminum sp.	Jasmine
Lapageria albiflora	Chilean Bellflower
Passiflora caerulea 'Constance Elliott'	Passionflower
Plumbago capensis album	White Leadwort
Polygonum aubertii	Silverlace Vine
Solanum jasminoides	Potato Vine
Stephanotis floribunda	Madagascar Jasmine
Swainsona galegifolia 'Albiflora'	Swan Flower
Trachelospermum jasminoides	Confederate, Star Jasmine

White (Hardy)

Anredera cordifolia	Madeira Vine
Calonyction aculeatum (Ipomoea alba)	Moonflower
Clematis flammula	Plumb Clematis
Clematis henryi	Henry Clematis
Clematis montana	Anemone Clematis
Clematis paniculata	Sweet Autumn Clematis
Clematis virginiana	Virgin's Bower
Cobaea scandens alba	White Coral Bells
Decumaria barbara	American Climbing Hydrangea
Dolichos lablab	Hyacinth Bean
Echinocystis lobata	Wild Cucumber
Hydrangea petiolaris	Climbing Hydrangea
Lathyrus latifolius 'White Pearl'	Perennial Sweet Pea
Lathyrus odoratus	Sweet Pea
Lonicera japonica	Japanese Honeysuckle
Polygonum aubertii	Silverlace Vine
Quamoclit pennata	Cypress Vine
Schizophragma hydrangioides	Climbing Hydrangea
Thunbergia alata	Black-Eyed Susan Vine
Wisteria sinensis alba	White Chinese Wisteria

***Trachelospermum jasminoides*, Star Jasmine**

Lavender (Tender)
Cymbalaria muralis	Kenilworth Ivy
Passiflora altaocaerulea	Pfordt Passionvine
Petrea volubilis	Queen's Wreath
Phaseolus caracalla	Snailvine

Lavender (Hardy)
Clematis crispa	Curly Clematis
Cobaea scandens	Coral Bells
Dolichos lablab	Hyacinth Bean

HOW TO USE VINES

Bougainvillea

**Distictis buccinatoria,
Blood-Red Trumpet Creeper**

Orange (Tender)

Campsis grandiflora	Chinese Trumpet Creeper
Pyrostegia venusta	Flamevine
Quisqualis indica	Rangoon Creeper
Senecio confusus	Mexican Flame Vine
Streptosolen jamesonii	Streptosolen
Thunbergia gibsonii	Orange Clockvine

Orange (Hardy)

Bignonia capreolata	Crossvine
Campsis radicans	Trumpet Creeper
Eccremocarpus scaber	Chilean Glory Flame
Lonicera sempervirens	Coral Honeysuckle

Red (Tender)

Bougainvillea 'Barbara Karst', 'Crimson Lake'	Bougainvillea
Clerodendron thompsoniae	Bleeding Heart Glorybower
Clianthus formosus	Glory Pea
Clianthus puniceus	Parrot's Bill
Gloriosa rothschildiana	Rothschild Glory Lily
Gloriosa superba	Malabar Glory Lily
Manettia inflata	Brazilian Firecracker
Passiflora jamesonii	Jameson Passionvine
Passiflora manicata	Red Passionflower
Passiflora racemosa	Princeps Passionvine
Passiflora quadrangularis	Giant Grandilla
Plumbago iudica	Scarlet Plumbago
Swainsona galegifolia	Swan Flower

Red (Hardy)

Antigonon leptopus	Coral Vine
Campsis sp.	Trumpet Creeper
Distictis buccinatoria	Blood Red Trumpet Vine
Clematis texensis	Scarlet Clematis
Clematis 'Mme Edouard André', 'Ville de Lyon'	Clematis
Ipomoea 'Scarlett O'Hara'	Morning Glory

Ipomoea setosa	Brazilian Morning Glory
Lonicera periclymenum belgica	Dutch Woodbine
Lonicera sempervirens 'Superba'	Scarlet Trumpet Honeysuckle
Lonicera heckrottii	Coral Honeysuckle
Phaseolus coccineus	Scarlet Runner Bean
Quamoclit pennata	Cypress Vine
Quamoclit lobata	Mina
Quamoclit sloteri	Cardinal Climber
Tropaeolum majus	Nasturtium

Violet to Purple (Tender)

Aristolochia elegans	Calico Flower
Aristolochia grandiflora	Pelican Flower
Bougainvillea glabra	Bougainvillea
Clytostoma callistegioides	Argentine Trumpet Vine
Distictis laxiflora	Vanilla Trumpet Vine
Dolichos lignosus	Australian Pea
Petrea volubilis	Queen's Wreath
Vinca major	Periwinkle

Violet to Purple (Hardy)

Clematis jackmanii	Jackman Clematis
Clematis viticella 'Purpurea'	Italian Clematis
Cobaea scandens	Coral Bells, Cathedral Bells
Lycium halimifolium	Matrimony Vine
Glechoma hederacea	Ground Ivy
Solanum dulcamara	Bitter Nightshade
Vinca minor	Dwarf Periwinkle
Wisteria floribunda	Japanese Wisteria
Wisteria sinensis	Chinese Wisteria

Clematis sp.

HOW TO USE VINES

Pink to Rose (Tender)

Antigonon leptopus	Love Vine
Bauhinia corymbosa	Phanera
Dipladenia splendens (*Manderilla splendens*)	Dipladenia
Ipomoea horsfalliae	Horsfall Morning Glory
Lapageria rosea	Chilean Bellflower
Passiflora jamesonii	Jameson Passionvine
Passiflora mollissima	Banana Passionfruit

Pink to Rose (Hardy)

Adlumia fungosa	Alleghany Vine
Clematis montana 'Rubens'	Pink Anemone Clematis
Lathyrus odoratus	Sweet Pea
Passiflora incarnata	Maypop Passionvine
Polygonum baldschuanicum	Bokara Vine
Schizophragma hydrangioides	Climbing Hydrangea
Wisteria sp.	Wisteria

Yellow (Tender)

Abutilon magapotamicum	Brazilian Abutilon
Adenocalymna inundatum	Loveflower
Allamanda hendersonii	Loveflower-of-Guiana
Hibbertia scandens	Gold Guinea Plant
Jasminum sp.	Jasmine
Macfadyena unguis-cati	Cat's Claw
Othonna capensis	Little-Pickles
Senecio mikanioides	German Ivy
Solandra maxima	Cup-of-Gold Vine
Stigmaphyllon ciliatum	Orchid Vine

Jasminum polyanthum,
Chinese Jasmine

Yellow (Hardy)

Clematis orientalis	Oriental Clematis
Clematis tangutica	Golden Clematis
Forsythia suspensa	Weeping Goldenbells
Lonicera japonica	Japanese Honeysuckle
Lonicera periclymenum	Dutch Honeysuckle
Lonicera sempervirens 'Sulphurea'	Yellow Trumpet Honeysuckle
Lonicera tellmanniana	Tellman Honeysuckle
Lysimachia nummularia	Creeping Jenny
Rosa sp.	Roses
Thunbergia alata	Black-Eyed Susan Vine
Tropaeolum majus	Nasturtium
Tropaeolum peregrinum	Canary Creeper
Trachelospermum asiaticum	Yellow Star Jasmine

***Rosa* 'High Noon'**

Blue (Tender)

Clitoria ternatea	Butterfly Pea
Hardenbergia comptoniana	Lilac Vine
Ipomoea leari	Blue Dawnflower
Jacquemontia pentantha	Jacquemontia
Maurandia barclaiana	Maurandia
Passiflora caerulea	Bluecrown Passionflower
Plumbago auriculata	Cape Leadwort
Solanum seaforthianum	Brazilian Nightshade
Solanum wendlandii	Paradise Flower
Thunbergia grandiflora	Bengal Clockvine
Thunbergia laurifolia	Laurel Clockvine

Blue (Hardy)

Clematis viticella	Italian Clematis
Ipomoea 'Heavenly Blue'	Morning Glory

3

Hardy Vines

Vines and other plants that can survive several days of weather during which the air temperature descends below 32°F (0°C) are called hardy. Sometimes these plants are simply referred to as "cold tolerant" or "winter hardy."

A few of these rugged vines are evergreen (English Ivy, *Hedera helix*; Wintercreeper, *Euonymus fortunei*), but the majority are deciduous species, perennial vines, and vinelike plants whose foliage withers with the first frost or freeze. Even though the latter, with their denuded, brittle stems, appear to be dead, dormant life in the roots will send up vigorous new growth with the first breath of spring.

Historically, plant hardiness has been determined by empirical knowledge, or trial and error. Plants that are native to one region are obviously acclimated to the prevailing climatic conditions in that area. But, when they are moved farther north to a colder zone, they may or may not survive. The same technique is used for exotic (imported) species. They are first trialed in regions that have temperature ranges and other climatic conditions similar to their native habitat. Then these limits may be pushed by testing their hardiness in colder areas, as well as their tolerance of more temperate environments.

It is a fact of horticultural life that, the farther south one goes in the U.S., the greater the selection of vines that grow successfully. The most reliable sources of information on which vines will prosper in a specific region are local nurserymen and county agricultural extension agents.

Hardiness is often variable. There are pockets of milder winter temperatures within a zonal region that permit the culture of plants normally restricted to warmer areas. These microclimates exist in nearly every part of the country and, in fact, the world. Also, one can adopt special techniques for protecting vines that are only marginally hardy in a particular geographic zone (see Chapter 9).

Many vines that are designated hardy may suffer some cold damage if they have not produced hard-wood and if their roots are not protected from ground freezes.

Listed below are vines that are winter hardy (32°F and below) with their northern zonal limitation in the U.S. noted in parentheses. This list is not a complete roster of hardy vines and vinelike plants that exist in cultivation. Those that are difficult to find in the trade have been excluded. Popularity of species waxes and wanes. Many of the plants that were avidly collected a few years ago have lost their appeal and become scarce.

Actinidia sp.

Actinidia kolomikta, Kolomikta Actinidia (4) is a decorative accent vine that is the least vigorous of the Actinidias and only reaches 15′. It is grown principally for the handsome variegated foliage of the male plants. Not bothered by pests or disease.
Flowers/Fruit: Produces ¾″ long white flowers with yellow anthers, in spring.
Foliage: Young leaves of male plants develop pink, red, white, and cream vegetation if grown in good light.
Height/Habit: To 15′. Twining climber.
Culture: Some shade during the hottest part of the day is essential, especially for young vines. Growth is best in fertile soil rich in humus that is kept evenly moist.
Uses: One of the best vines for creating dense shade when grown on arbors and trellises. Does well on wire grids and wrought-iron fences as a summer screen.
Propagation: Seed, cuttings, and layering. Cuttings should be taken in summer from new wood, or in the fall from ripened wood. Root in moist sand, vermiculite, and milled peat moss.
Pruning: If needed for control or training, prune in fall or early spring.

A. polygama, Silvervine (4), could well be called the "catnip climber" since cats are attracted to it and have been known to destroy the vine by mauling and clawing it. New plants should be protected by hardware cloth or chicken wire screening until they are well established. Young stems need to be anchored and trained to climb. It bears fragrant white flowers 1″ in diameter that have either brown or yellow anthers, but blooms are often hidden by the plant's dense foliage. Male Silvervines have leaves with a silver-white tinge that is the source of the plant's common name although more mature foliage may be spotted or splotched with yellow. It twines like *A. kolomikta* with twining stems, but attains greater heights. Its propagation and pruning requirements are the same.

Akebia quinata, Five-Leaf Akebia (4)   A graceful, desirable Oriental import that is native to China, Japan, and Korea adapts well to all but the northern extremes of the U.S. It is evergreen in temperate climates, deciduous in cold-winter regions, but holds its leaves well into winter. A rapid, vigorous grower that is largely disease- and pest-free.

Flowers/Fruit: As early as April, clusters of small cupped flowers emitting a pleasant, spicy fragrance appear. Both male and female flowers are borne in the same cluster. Male flowers are rosy, purplish-brown; female blossoms are purplish violet-brown with three petals. In its native habitats, plant produces cloyingly sweet purple fruit that is full of seeds, in the fall. To force Akebia to fruit in non-native environments, flowers must be hand-pollinated.

Foliage: Leaves are compound and comprised of five dark green leaflets about 2″ long, joined by stems.

Height/Habit: To 30′. Twining climber.

Culture: Quite adaptable species that thrives in a warm, sun-drenched spot, but does nicely in the shade. Best plants are grown in light, humusy, well-drained soil. Heavy and alkaline media should be improved.

Uses: An attractive choice where light shade is wanted or where the effect of delicate design tracery is desired. Can be used as a screening plant on fences, trellises, and lathwork.

Akebia quinata, **Five-Leaf Akebia**

Propagation: By seed, cuttings, layering, or root division. Cuttings may be taken from old or new (current season) wood, and the latter should have two leaves left on cutting. Seeds germinate readily in moist sand and vermiculite.

Pruning: Because Akebia can become rank if not controlled, it requires annual pruning—primarily, heading back—especially in mild-winter regions where growth is not checked by harsh weather. Recovers rapidly, even when taken back to the ground.

Ampelopsis aconitifolia, Monkshood Vine (4)
This attractive, gracefully growing vine is slow to produce much growth the first season or two. It then makes up for lost time, becoming a vigorous plant that needs annual pruning to keep it in check.
Flowers/Fruit: Blooms are small, greenish, and insignificant. Grown for its decorative fruits—small berries that turn from greenish yellow to bright blue.
Foliage: Five-segmented leaves, 2″–3″ long, with each lobe divided, somewhat resembling a maple leaf.
Height/Habit: To 20′. Tendril climber.
Culture: Sun to partial shade. Not particular about soil, but prospers in a humusy, well-drained medium.
Uses: Excellent choice for shade on trellises or arbors and as a ground cover.
Propagation: Seed, cuttings, and layers. Take softwood cuttings in July and hardwood cuttings in September. Propagation is hastened under glass. Seeds can be germinated in moist sand, vermiculite, and milled peat moss.
Pruning: Thin, shape, and head back in early spring.

A. brevipedunculata is a related species that is a strong, rapid grower. It is both cold tolerant and resistant to wind damage. Like the Monkshood Vine, the colorful fruits it bears make it an appealing specimen plant when displayed in a prominent location. Its berrylike fruits are ¼″ in diameter and change from lavender to turquoise-green to bright blue and finally to black, in late summer or early fall. Leaves are 5″ wide with three coarsely toothed lobes. Its only drawbacks are its susceptibility to leaf spot and the fact that caterpillars have an affinity for it. Leaf spot can be controlled by snipping off and discarding (not in the compost pile) infected leaves, then spraying the plant with Bordeaux mix (copper sulfate and hydrated lime). See Chapter 9 for organic controls of caterpillars. Provide the same basic care as for *A. aconitifolia.*

Aristolochia durior, Dutchman's Pipe (4) Ideal for quickly covering porches, latticework, walls (even north-facing walls), arbors, and pergolas where deep shade is desired or seasonal screening of unappealing views is sought. No vine performs these tasks better than Dutchman's Pipe with its heavy mat of overlapping foliage. Although growth is modest to start, the vine soon takes off with rampant growth rivalling the notorious kudzu. Occasionally plagued by caterpillars, but otherwise problem-free, even tolerating urban pollution. A strong support is needed.
Flowers/Fruit: Blooms are 1½″–3″ wide, tubular, malodorous, yellowish, purple, or brown, and shaped like a calabash pipe—the source of the vine's common

Aristolochia durior, **Dutchman's Pipe**

name. Flowers may appear singly or in clusters and are usually hidden under a mantle of foliage. Fruits are capsulelike and insignificant.

Foliage: Large (6″–14″) heart- or kidney-shaped glossy-green leaves that overlap to produce a water-shedding, deep-shade-producing mat.

Height/Habit: After a slow start, vine rapidly climbs to 30′ or more. Twining climber.

Culture: Forgiving of adverse conditions, Dutchman's Pipe will thrive with weedlike abandon in virtually any soil or exposure. Even moisture spurs better growth. Young plants in their maiden year need protection in harsh-winter regions.

Uses: Provides deepest shade for any location and serves well as a seasonal screen plant that may remain mostly evergreen in mild climates.

Propagation: Seed, cuttings, and layers. Take cuttings of ripened wood in late summer. Seeds germinate well in moist sand and vermiculite.

Pruning: If desired, thin and head back in spring or summer.

There are two tender varieties for outdoor growing in frost-free areas of Florida and California, or greenhouse culture everywhere: Calico Flower (*A. elegans*) and Pelican Flower (*A. grandiflora* 'Sturtevantii').

Campsis radicans (also known as *Bignonia radicans* and *Tecoma radicans*), Trumpet Creeper (4) Although seldom chosen as a decorative garden plant in the southeastern U.S., where it is considered as something of a rampant weed, *C. radicans* is widely planted and admired in the rest of the country, prospering in a broad zonal range. Its vividly hued flowers can add a splash of color where it is needed for most of the summer. Aphids occasionally are a problem, but these can be controlled with insecticidal soap or spritzing with the garden hose.

Flowers/Fruit: Red-orange, 3″ long trumpet-shaped blooms in terminal clusters of six to twelve appear in July and continue on until September. Cultivars with other floral colors include *C. atropurpurea* (all scarlet flowers) and *C. flava* (yellow blooms).

Foliage: Leaves are dark green, compound, and opposite and comprised of 9–11 leaflets 1½″–2½″ long.

Height/Habit: Quick growth to 50′, although 35′ is average. Clinging climber (aerial rootlets). While rootlets anchor efficiently to flat surfaces, this vine is rampant and heavy and occasionally needs to have its stems lashed to a strong support (wire, trellis) to prevent the plant from collapsing under its own weight.

Culture: Ideal conditions include a sunny exposure to encourage floral production, and moist, humus-rich soil. But *C. radicans* is tolerant of neglect, imperfect conditions, and wind if well-anchored.

Uses: Because the vine is barren during the winter months, it is often relegated to less prominent sites, such as fences and outbuildings, where it provides both cover and color.

Propagation: Seed, cuttings, and layers. Seeds should be germinated in sandy loam or vermiculite and sand under glass in a warm spot. Cuttings of last year's growth (mature wood) should be taken in early spring and rooted under glass with bottom heat.

Pruning: Stems require shortening and thinning annually to groom the plant and encourage new, vigorous growth. Unrestrained pruning, though, can reduce floral production, since the plant blooms on current-season wood. To keep bald areas from developing and to promote lusher growth, pinch out growing tips periodically during the summer.

Although similar in many respects to *C. radicans*, the native American species, Chinese Trumpet Creeper (*C. grandiflora chinensis*) is more restrained in growth and is intolerant of the bitterly cold winters prevalent in the extreme north. Conversely, it finds the torrid heat of the low desert areas of the American West much to its liking. From July to September it bears scarlet blooms that are somewhat larger than those of *C. radicans*. The lips of the corolla flare to 3″ in diameter, and it attains about 20′ of height. Some tying off to supports is usually required to train the vine. A more popular hybrid between *C. g. chinensis* and *C. radicans* is *C.* × *tagliabuana* 'Madame Galen', which bears loose clusters of salmon-red flowers, is as

Campsis radicans, **Trumpet Creeper**

cold-hardy as any of the *Campsis* species, and grows to 30′.

Celastrus scandens, American Bittersweet (4) This native American species is grown primarily for its abundant, colorful, berrylike fruit that clings to the stems all winter, and also for the striking yellow tinge the foliage takes on in the fall, just before the leaves drop. Bittersweets are not well-mannered vines. They tend to be invasive and are best restricted to remote sections of the garden where their tendency to gobble up real estate doesn't create a problem. A sturdy support will be needed to carry the weight of this vigorous vine. Unless the sex of the plant is known when purchased, several should be set in to guarantee efficient pollination and fruit production.

Some plants produce only male flowers, which do not produce fruit; some bear only fruit-forming female flowers, which need a male nearby for pollination. Others may have both male and female blooms on the same vine; still others may produce perfect flowers containing both pollen-bearing anthers (male) and pollen-receiving stigmas within the pistil (female). With practice, grafting can produce self-sufficient plants carrying both male and female flowers.

Flowers/Fruit: In June, insignificant creamy-white to greenish-white, scentless flowers appear in 2″–4″ long terminal clusters. Female plants produce yellowish-orange, berrylike fruits about ⅓″ in diameter along stems. Berries split open in the fall to display the bright red arils enclosing the seeds. These persist on the stems through the winter, providing a colorful accent and forage for birds.

Foliage: Leaves are 2″–4″ long with toothed margins, a handsome lime-green color turning yellow before dropping in the fall.

Height/Habit: To 20′. Twining climber.

Culture: Bittersweet thrives in sunny to partially shady situations and is not bothered by wind. Although the ideal medium is a moist, slightly acid, well-drained loam, it adapts to a variety of soil compositions. It fails in boggy soil and heavy peat, but takes occasional drought in stride. Plants newly set in should be drastically cut back. Initial heavy pruning results in more vigorous and productive plants.

Uses: Due to its rank growth, plant should be relegated to outer walls and fences where its takeover tendency can be tolerated. Bittersweets merrily scamper over inhospitable and rocky terrain and quickly cover banks.

Propagation: Cuttings and layers. Cuttings of ripe and softwood should be taken in winter. Root hardwood cuttings in a mix of one part milled peat moss to four parts sand, with bottom heat. Softwood roots without heating cables.

Pruning: Prune to shape and take out dead wood in late winter or early spring before growth starts. Bear in mind that fruit forms on current season's wood, much like grapes.

Two other Bittersweets that are desirable for the home garden are Anglestem Bittersweet (*C. angulatus*) and Oriental Bittersweet (*C. orbiculatus*), which grows to 40′. Culture requirements and zonal range are the same as for *C. scandens.*

***Clematis* sp.** Most of these handsome and diverse vines seen in gardens today are cultivars of imported species. Breeders have produced over 100 improved cultivars that are easier to grow and more floriferous than their parents. Even so, Clematis is not a foolproof vine, but neither is it as difficult as its reputation among some gardeners would indicate. It has some specific needs that are simple to supply, and its beauty and versatility make it well worth the extra care.

Grown for its long-lived flowers, a delightful variety of shapes, sizes, and colors are available. Hues range from subtle to bold shades of pink, blue, lavender, and purple, with some sepals accented with contrasting bars. And for shady situations and night gardens, there are pure whites that almost glow in the dark.

General cultural requirements that enhance your chances for success are:

(1) Select a type that is zoned for your specific geographic region. If, for example, you garden in the northern U.S. where winters are severe, you can't successfully grow *Clematis armandii*, which has a zonal limit of 8 year-round outdoors. You *can* confine it to a container and bring it indoors for the winter, but—for a permanent species for the garden—*C. jouiniana* or, possibly, *C. texensis* will adapt happily to your climatic conditions.

(2) Choose the right site. A prevalent maxim counsels gardeners to grow Clematis with its head in the sun and its feet in the shade. Obviously, this is not an easy goal to achieve. The point is that Clematis roots need to be protected from the deleterious effects of the summer sun. One can do this by growing the plants in east- or north-facing sites, establishing perennials near them that shade their crowns, growing ground covers around them, and by maintaining a deep layer of mulch where they are planted.

(3) Prepare the planting site by cultivating the soil deeply so that roots are not compacted and there is good aeration around them.

(4) Amend overly acidic or alkaline soil. Clematises thrive in soil that is slightly alkaline to neutral on the pH scale (7.0). If your soil is acidic, work in sufficient agricultural-grade lime to create a neutral medium. Overly alkaline soil may be amended with milled peat moss.

(5) Set transplants in so their crowns are 2″–3″ below grade to protect the delicate young stems and provide good insulation for their sensitive roots. This is especially important for grafted specimens, which must be planted deeply enough to cover the scion-stock union. Although this is counter to common garden practice with grafted trees, it is standard in the culture of Clematises. Rooting from the grafted section that is induced helps sustain the vine and spurs it to produce more blooms and better growth. Clematis vines that are planted too high will often die back.

Most Clematises are sold in containers and, once the plants are knocked out (taking care not to damage the stems, which are easily broken), they should be planted with the soil ball enclosing the roots intact. Mail order vines are normally shipped bare root. After soaking these in a bucket of water overnight, they should be planted on a mound of soil built up in a planting hole that is wide enough to accommodate splaying the roots out horizontally in a natural growing pattern. Cramped roots usually yield fewer and smaller flowers.

Trellises or other supports on which Clematis vines will be trained should be anchored in the ground *before* vines are planted to obviate root and stem damage. Firm the backfill soil around the root ball, water well to collapse air pockets, and cover the crown with a layer of organic mulch for added insulation.

(6) Don't cultivate the soil around Clematis vines once they are established. Subsurface roots are vulnerable to damage. To protect the stems at ground level from mishap, install an enclosure of hardware cloth or chicken wire.

(7) Keep soil evenly moist but not boggy. Clematises are vigorous growers and require ample water with perfect drainage during the growing season. Opinions vary on whether fertilizer is beneficial. Organics that are low in nitrogen, such as well-rotted (composted) cow manure, can be used as a top dressing and watered in if vines appear to lack energy.

Propagation is accomplished by cuttings, layers, and grafts. Grafting requires skill and experience and may not be a technique the average gardener would want to undertake. Softwood cuttings taken in early summer root easily in damp vermiculite and sand.

Well-grown Clematises are largely problem-free, although they may be plagued by stem rot resulting from injury to stem tissue or shallow planting. This condition is irreversible and infected plants should be destroyed. Another fungal disease that takes its toll on plants grown in humid conditions is Clematis wilt. This too has no cure. Occasionally, snipping off the plant at the soil line will spur new growth from underground stems.

Aphids can be a problem, but one that is easily dealt with either by spritzing plants (both sides of the leaves and the blooms) with a gentle spray from the garden hose or by using insecticidal soap in a misting bottle.

Following are a few of the popular Clematises well worth collecting:

C. armandii, Evergreen Clematis (8) One of the most useful vines in regions with milder winters, Evergreen Clematis is an excellent year-round foliage plant with the added bonus of a brief flowering period in late spring. White flowers, 1½″–2½″ broad, are copiously produced in clusters held above the foliage. These are followed by long, plumed seed pods. Foliage is glossy green, ovate or lanceolate, opposite, and composed of three leaflets 3″–6″ long on drooping petioles. Vine may reach 25′ after a slow start. Blooms on previous season's wood, so pruning should be done after flowers fade. Use anywhere a mantle of green is desired: over pergolas and arbors, along eaves and fences, and on trellises for screening. A frost-tender variety, *C. a.* var. Farquhariana 'Apple Blossom', bears 2″ wide pale pink flowers.

C. jackmanii, Jackman Clematis (5), is one of the more popular of the large-flowered cultivars and hybrids. Its blossoms are really rays of sepals radiating from a core of pistils and stamens. These average 6″ in width, but—in well-grown specimens—8″ is common. Species flowers are an intense velvety purple, but cultivars offer a variety of hues. Some of the best among these are 'Comtesse de Bouchard' (pink); 'Henryi' (white); 'Mme Edouard André' (scarlet-purple); 'Mrs. Cholmondeley' (light lavender-blue); and 'Rubra' (intense pink).

Clematis jackmanii 'Mrs. Cholmondeley'

Jackman Clematises grow to 15′ with wiry, twisting stems and are useful on arbors, fences, trellises, and walls. Flowers are produced (July to October) on the current season's wood, so fall is the time for heading the vine back. Winter kills it to the ground, but protected roots produce vigorous new stems in spring.

C. paniculata (*C. dioscoreifolia robusta*), Sweet Autumn Clematis (5), has fragrant white flowers 1″–1½″ wide borne in panicles, from about late July to October. These are followed by decorative seed heads. Leaves are ovate and compound, comprised of three leaflets, and have a leathery texture. Maximum height is 30′, and it also is a handsome ground cover. Ideal for arbors and trellises close to the house where its floral display and aroma can be appreciated. May be largely evergreen in mild-winter regions and sheltered nooks.

Clematis jackmanii, Jackman Clematis

C. texensis, Scarlet Clematis (5) is considered by many devotees to be the most attractive of our native Clematises. It is thought to have originated in Texas and, in character with other wild plants of that largely semi-arid region, is surprisingly drought tolerant, although it thrives in evenly moist media. Flowers are stalked, bright scarlet, 1″ long, bell- or urn-shaped, and profuse, from July to early November. Well-grown vines are ablaze with color and should be isolated to an area where their floral show won't be diluted by competing with other flowering species. Blossoms are followed by interesting seed pods that open to release highly decorative silvery plumes. Foliage is glossy bluish-green with up to eight leaflets 2″–3½″ long. Blooms on current season's wood and may quickly grow to about 10′. Two choice varieties are 'Duchess of Albany' (pink with brown center) and 'Countess of Onslow', or 'Comtesse de Onslow' (violet-purple with a scarlet band).

***Dioscorea batatus*,** Cinnamonvine, Chinese Yam (5)   There are mixed feelings in the gardening world regarding this novel plant. To many people, it is a rank, invasive weed; to others, it is an interesting and worthwhile vine. An edible tuber (grown as a food source in the tropics), it produces a tangle of twining stems. Relatively pest- and disease-free, it dies to the ground with the first frost but recovers in the spring.

Flowers/Fruit: Blooms are small, white, produced in clusters, and have the appealing fragrance of cinnamon. Fruits are edible tubers formed in the leaf axils in the fall. If not harvested, they occasionally drop to the ground and root, which is the method the plant uses to propagate itself in the wild.

Foliage: Opposite, somewhat heart-shaped, glossy dark green leaves on short stems, from 2″–4″ long.

Height/Habit: To 31′. Twining climber.

Culture: Requires minimal care and prospers both in shady and sunny situations and in a wide variety of soils, provided they drain well. Although hardy to Zone 5, the tuber can be killed by prolonged hard freezes and should be given protection in harsh-winter areas or dug and stored until spring.

Uses: Its thick foliage mat makes this vine suitable for providing shade on porches and arbors. Because of its rank habit, it is probably best in remote areas of the garden.

Propagation: Seed, cuttings, and (easiest) rooting small bulblets, or tubers.

Pruning: Common practice is to prune back stems to the ground in fall.

***Euonymus fortunei radicans*,** American Bittersweet, Evergreen Wintercreeper (5)   Formerly known as *Euonymus radicans* and still sold under that name by many plantsmen, this is the most adaptable and desirable evergreen vine for northern climes. Although its zonal limitation is listed as 5, it will survive and prosper in many portions of Zone 4 if planted in sheltered locations out of the path of harsh, dessicating winter winds, and given a deep mulch blanket for winter protection. It offers a durable option to English Ivy (*Hedera helix*) in the north and in parts of New England where even ivy must be grown only as a ground cover. It is a moderately slow grower that needs some support and direction to climb, and may only attain 10′ feet of height after years of tending. Still, its neat, even mat of green makes the wait worthwhile.

A serious threat to the health of Wintercreepers, especially in the northeastern and central regions of the country, is Euonymus scale, which appears on foliage and stems as small bumps, primarily on leaf undersides. These destructive pests extract sap from plants, causing leaves to turn yellow and stems to die back. Control is difficult unless caught early. Small, initial invasions can be repulsed by scraping off scales with one's fingernail, then spraying the affected area with superior oil—sometimes called summer oil—during the growing season, and dormant oil in the winter. If scales have established a beachhead before they are discovered, prune out infested wood and apply the

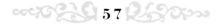

appropriate oil. As a preventive measure, spray healthy plants in winter with dormant oil and twice during the summer with a superior oil.

Flowers/Fruit: Insignificant greenish-white flowers in axillary clusters in late June. Fruits are either greenish-white or pink-tinged, and split open in fall to display orange, berrylike seeds that cling until the first frost.

Foliage: Leaves are ovate, opposite, 1″–2″ long, thick, leathery, and a deep, glossy green. Some may be accented with white.

Height/Habit: To 25′ with maturity, but 15′ is average. Clinging climber with rootlike holdfasts.

Culture: Better growth and quicker maturity is achieved if plant is grown in full sun. Performs well (but more slowly) in shade. Bitter winds can "burn" foliage, but vine is tolerant of warmer zephyrs. Best specimens are grown in evenly moist media in which well-rotted manure has been worked in at planting time and as a top dressing/mulch in spring. Needs sturdy support and guidance to climb.

Uses: Wall/fence covering, accent, ground cover.

Propagation: Cutting and layers. Cuttings of half-ripened wood (current season's growth) taken in summer or fall may be rooted in a mix of moist sand and milled peat moss in a shaded cold frame or under plastic or glass. Branches may be layered in late June.

Pruning: Pruning is usually done in early spring to train the vine and remove dead wood diseased or scale-infested portions or errant branches.

Curiously, the mature form of *E. f. radicans* is known as *E. f.* 'Carrieri'. Along with the name change come alterations in the plant's character at maturity—larger leaves and longer, woodier branches, more abundant flowers and fruits, the latter produced in clusters.

In many regions, a host of varieties and cultivars are available that are more familiar to and popular with gardeners than the species. One of the best of these is Big-Leaf Wintercreeper (*E. f. vegeta*), which only grows to 4′–5′. Its leaves are a bit larger and

rounder. Flowers are more abundant and the fruits that follow—clusters of orangish berries—are persistent through the winter, adding a bright accent in an otherwise colorless season. These fruits, which are the seeds of the vine, may be propagated, but the resulting plants will be barren of fruit. New growth in spring is an attractive chartreuse.

Another handsome version is the Purple-Leaf Wintercreeper (*E. f.* 'Colorata'), which doesn't climb and is primarily used as a ground cover. It will spread across a flat surface such as a wall with guidance. Both plants have basically the same culture requirements and zonal limitations as *E. f. radicans*.

Hedera helix, English Ivy (4) England's most popular evergreen climber is also widely admired in America, where many of its 100+ varieties were developed. English Ivy is one of the most versatile vines—perhaps *the* most versatile, since its handsome, tidy foliage and compact habit make it useful in draping walls and fences, covering slopes and topiary frames, and as a house and outdoor container plant. Although it is marginal in Zone 4, three cultivars are more cold-tolerant: 'Baltica', which has smaller leaves with striking white veins; 'Bulgaria', widely seen in New England gardens; and 'Romania'. Spider mites

Hedera helix, **English Ivy**

and mealybugs occasionally infest it, but these are easily controlled with insecticidal soap and other organic measures.

Flowers/Fruit: Insignificant green flowers in umbels are produced only on mature plants. Fruits are small, black berries.

Foliage: Immature vines have wedge-shaped leaves, 2"–5" long, with 3–5 lobes. As the plant matures, leaves lose their lobes and become squarish. Mature branches, which don't cling, form when they are permitted to grow out from a clinging stem. This can be avoided by pruning out errant branches. Other varieties have leaves of different shapes and markings, including variegation (Gold Leaf Ivy, *H. h.* 'Aureo-variegata').

Height/Habit: To 80', although 50' is average. Clinging climber with aerial rootlets.

Culture: Grows best in partial to full shade. Sun may bleach or scorch leaves. Prefers moist, humusy soil, but established vines are fairly drought tolerant. If foliage of shaded plants begins to yellow, feed with an organic nitrogen fertilizer in spring. In marginal zones, restrict *H. helix* to north-facing situations to minimize winter damage from cutting winds.

Uses: Wall and fence coverings, screens, ground cover, topiary, specimen plant.

Propagation: Cuttings and layers. Cuttings with two or three aerial roots attached may be taken during the growing season and rooted in moist sand and milled peat moss.

Pruning: Pinch back growing tips periodically to promote new, vigorous growth and to keep vine compact and bushy. Neglected plants should be pruned back hard and sheared in early spring to control and achieve desired effect. *H. helix* can't be overpruned.

Hydrangea petiolaris, Climbing Hydrangea (5)
This glorious vine with its snowy white flowers and dense foliage can be grown much farther north than its zonal limitation, even up to southern Canada, since it is quite tolerant of cold. It is a fine choice for cov-

Hedera helix, 'Pixie', English Ivy

ering broad, high expanses of rough-surface walls quickly, after it is well established. Like most clingers with holdfasts, it should not be used on wood if there are concerns about surface damage. It is generally pest- and disease-free.

Flowers/Fruit: In late June or early July, Climbing Hydrangea bears broad clusters of attractive, pure white blossoms that are carried on long stems.

Foliage: Leaves are 2"–4" long, heart-shaped with serrated edges, bright shiny green, and change to gold in fall. When leaves drop, the plant's handsome shredding red bark is visible.

Height/Habit: To 50'+. Clinging climber with aerial rootlets.

Culture: Set plants in a location that provides partial (not deep) shade to full sun, to encourage greater floral production and vigorous growth. Prospers in deep, moist, fertile loam enhanced with rich compost that drains well.

Uses: Ideal candidate for large expanses of brick, stone, or stucco. Requires a solid surface for rootlets to anchor themselves to or vine tends to collapse and ramble.

Propagation: Cuttings (difficult) and layers (easy).

Pruning: Requires minimal pruning and then only to thin and maintain appearance. Neglected vines and those that lack energy or produce few blossoms may be pruned heavily in winter or early spring to rejuvenate.

Two similar species, but not so hardy as *H. petiolaris*, are *Decumaria barbara*, Southeast Climbing Hydrangea, which blooms a month earlier, and *Schizophragma hydrangeoides*, Japanese Hydrangea Vine, which bears pinkish-white flowers in clusters 6"–8" broad and only grows to about 30' high. Both have culture requirements and uses similar to those of *H. petiolaris*, but *D. barbara* should have winter protection if grown much beyond its zonal limit.

Lonicera **sp.,** Honeysuckle Of the many honeysuckles in cultivation, the four species and two cultivars listed below are hardy enough to tolerate freezing temperatures and are useful in the home landscape. In addition to providing dense shade and decorative surface covers, most have long-lasting, sweetly scented flowers. Specific care for each species is given below. Propagation is generally by cuttings taken in late June and rooted in moist sand, vermiculite, and milled peat moss. Branches that are bent down and held on the surface of damp soil with a stone root freely.

Lonicera japonica, Japanese Honeysuckle (5) has sired offspring that exceed it in foliage mass and floral beauty, but it remains a useful (though sometimes overly rampant) vine. Scented flowers are white with a purple tinge, fading to yellow, 1"–1½" long, appearing in late spring. Foliage is ovate to oblong and 1"–3" long. Vine reaches 30' on twining stems. Tends to be unruly and may need hard pruning in fall or early spring (in the eastern U.S.) to keep it in check.

There are two superior varieties: *L. j. chinensis*, Chinese Purple Honeysuckle (5), which bears flowers and foliage fringed with purple. It has the same range and

growth potential as the species. *L. j.* 'Purpurea' is thought to be the same variety; *L. j.* 'Halliana', Hall's Honeysuckle (4), is a rampant evergreen grower that has naturalized in the wild in many areas and become a pest in some. It produces pairs of fragrant white flowers to 1½" long that change to pale yellow with age. Leaves are dense, 3"–4" long and take on a bronze-yellow hue in fall. It will quickly cover a fence, arbor, or slope and grows well under tree canopies. An amazingly adaptable plant, it thrives as far north as southern Canada and south to the subtropical regions of Florida. Evergreen to semi-evergreen depending on geographical area, it can attain 30' of height.

Lonicera hildebrandiana, Giant Burmese Honeysuckle (9) is a marginal vine in the hardy category that will bounce back from a heavy freeze, but is much more tolerant of heat than cold. Like Hall's Honeysuckle, it bears copious white aromatic tubular flowers that turn yellow with age, but the blossoms of *L. hildebrandiana* are up to 7" long. Flowering, which

Lonicera japonica 'Purpurea', Purple Honeysuckle

begins in early summer, may last for up to seven months in the ideal environment. Its evergreen (or semi-evergreen, depending on climate) leaves are ovate, glossy green, to 6″ long. The plant's thick, ropy, twining stems can carry it up a wall to 80′. It tolerates many types of soil, but prospers in humusy, evenly moist, well-drained loam. Arid soil and low humidity cause the vine to deteriorate. Use this one where a bold, tropical effect is desired.

Lonicera sempervirens, Trumpet Honeysuckle,

Lonicera sempervirens **'Magnifica', Magnificent Trumpet Honeysuckle**

Lonicera sempervirens**, Trumpet Honeysuckle**

Coral Honeysuckle (4+) is an attractive native of the northeastern U.S. that is easily adaptable to mild-winter areas, where it remains largely evergreen. Its scentless flowers are quite decorative 2″ long trumpets ranging from orange to coral and are displayed in terminal clusters. Blooming begins in early summer (late spring in warmer climates) and lasts into early fall. Leaves are not as showy as most others. They are opposite, oval to oblong, 2″–3″ long and are a dull blue-green on the upper surface. Scarlet berries appear in the fall. It grows to 50′ on twining stems, but 25′ is average. Tolerant of adverse conditions, soil composition, and drought (once established). Needs a strong support, and the best-looking specimens are usually ones that have been heavily thinned to remove woody stems and headed back in fall or early spring (in the north) to encourage bushier and more vigorous growth. Serves well as a seasonal screen, wall, or fence covering and, if allowed to sprawl, as an effective slope and ground cover (low to no traffic areas).

Lonicera tellmanniana, Tellman Honeysuckle (5) is a hybrid cross between *L. sempervirens* and *L. tragophylla.* It is a deciduous vine and resembles its one parent, Trumpet Honeysuckle, except that it bears clusters of flowers tipped with a pinkish or reddish-bronze blush, in summer. It can reach up to 35′ in height and needs a sturdy support. Use as a decorative accent on fences and wall trellises.

Menispermum canadense, Moonseed (3), is another of those plants that get mixed reviews from gardeners. To some, it is a nuisance because of its invasive habit of spreading, like raspberries, via underground stems, popping up in places where it is not welcome. To others, it is the perfect vine for rapidly covering a screen or barren stretch of rocky terrain where no well-mannered plant will go. Its common name derives from the crescent-moon shape of its seeds. No pests or diseases seriously threaten it.

Flowers/Fruit: Small, yellowish-white flowers that are hardly noticeable appear anytime from late spring to late summer. In the fall, female plants produce black fruits that resemble grapes.

Foliage: Abundantly produced leaves are 4″–8″ long, 4″–5″ in diameter, glossy dark green, 3–7 lobed or angled, and round to ovate. Their massed effect is a lush blanket of green.

Height/Habit: To 12′, although some grown under ideal conditions exceed the average. Twining climber.

Culture: Prospers in shade and moist (even wet) soil. Fails in hot, dry environments. Will grow in sun with ample water.

Uses: A good choice for damp, naturalized gardens and wildlife habitats, where its rampant growth is usually acceptable or even welcomed. Performs nicely on a light lattice against cool, shaded walls, and quickly covers stretches of rough terrain where ample moisture is present.

Propagation: Seed and cuttings. Start seed indoors in early spring in damp sand, vermiculite, and milled peat moss. Set seedlings out after frost danger has passed. Take cuttings of ripened wood in summer and root in same germination mix used for starting seed.

Pruning: None needed. Herbaceous stems die to the ground with the first hard frost. Recovers quickly in spring.

Parthenocissus tricuspidata, Boston Ivy, Japanese Creeper (5+) When it comes to covering walls, the undisputed champion in the deciduous division is Boston Ivy. It seems "designed" for the task, producing handsome and interesting foliage that overlaps like shingles to create a water-shedding mantle. In fall, its vivid golds and scarlets rival maples for beauty.

Flowers/Fruit: Insignificant flowers are produced in summer. These are followed by blue-black, grapelike berries that persist into winter.

Foliage: Either simple, with three sharply pointed, toothed lobes, or compound, composed of three leaflets. At maturity, leaves are from 4″–6″ across and

Parthenocissus tricuspidata, Boston Ivy

HARDY VINES

6″–9″ long. With the first cool weather, they begin to take on the fiery colors of fall.

Height/Habit: To 60′. Tendril climber with holdfasts.

Culture: Sunny or partially shady locations and evenly moist, humusy soil produce the best-looking plants, but Boston Ivy is tolerant of a variety of growing conditions and soil compositions.

Uses: Best on walls close to the house, where its fall fireworks can be appreciated. Use on any flat surface where its holdfasts won't create maintenance problems.

Propagation: Seed, cuttings, and layers. Although vines can be grown from seed, this involves a long wait. Seeds should be sown where plants are desired in prepared sites with fertile, deeply cultivated soil. Freezing aids germination. Cuttings and layers root readily and produce satisfactory plants faster.

Pruning: Seldom needed. For guidance, prune selectively in early spring.

Two choice varieties are available. Low's Japanese Creeper (*P. t.* 'Lowii') has much smaller rosettelike leaves just 1½″ long with deeper-cut lobes and is less vigorous. Veitch's Creeper (*P. t.* 'Veitchii'), the juvenile form of the species vine, produces even smaller leaves with a purple tinge and greenish flowers favored by honeybees. Both varieties are adaptable to a wide range of soil compositions and exposures, although partial shade and fertile, evenly moist media encourage vigorous, healthy vines. Both plants are occasionally targeted by Japanese beetles and plagued by mildew in overly humid or damp environments. (See Chapter 9 for controls.)

A slightly hardier related species is *Parthenocissus quinquefolia*, Virginia Creeper (4+), which, like Boston Ivy, is admired for its brilliantly hued fall foliage, which changes to golden crimson and scarlet. It is a vigorous grower that eventually climbs to 50′, especially on shaded walls. Its sparsely produced holdfast discs cling best to rough-textured surfaces. Flowers, borne in summer, are insignificant, but the blue-black, ½″ fruits, carried on red-stalked stems like grapes, are decorative in late summer. Leaves, which open

***Parthenocissus quinquefolia*, Virginia Creeper**

purplish, are composed of five leaflets with toothed margins, 2″–5″ long, elliptic to oblong. Vine produces side shoots which droop attractively on stems. Virginia Creeper has the same basic culture requirements as Boston Ivy. Use if for visual interest on walls and fences and for light-to-heavy shade on arbors and pergolas. Also a fine ground cover that roots readily where the joints contact the soil.

An equally hardy, denser-growing variety gaining popularity is Engelmann Ivy (*P. q.* 'Engelmanii'), which produces smaller leaves that are thick and leathery.

Periploca graeca, Silkvine (4+) This vine's common name comes from the silklike hairs that stud its flowers. It is a fine, fast-growing twining climber whose dark green foliage is quite attractive. Pests leave it alone and it is largely disease-free.

Flowers/Fruit: Bears 1″ wide, star-shaped flowers in summer that are brownish-purple above and greenish-yellow below. They are carried on long stems in clusters of up to a dozen. The blossoms emit a sweet aroma that is almost cloying and that many people find a bit nauseating after a while. Fruits are 5″ long seed pods that rupture to release fluffy seeds, in fall.

Foliage: Long, pointed, opposite, willowy leaves to 5″ long that are a deep, lustrous green.

Polygonum aubertii, Silverlace Vine

Height/Habit: Quickly ascends trellises and wires to 40′. Twining climber with stems that weave themselves together.

Culture: Sun and moist, humusy soil are the only requisites. Tolerant of cold and heat, mucky or arid media, and wind.

Uses: As an accent, temporary screen and shade covering for arbors, pergolas, and trellises. Requires a strong support to carry the weight of its mass at maturity.

Propagation: Cuttings and layers. Take cuttings of young growth in summer and root them in moist sand, vermiculite, and milled peat moss.

Pruning: If needed, head back in spring to direct growth.

Polygonum aubertii, Silverlace Vine, Fleeceflower (4) While many vines are grown for the beauty of their foliage, a few are prized for their floral splendor. Silverlace Vine is one of these, bearing long-lasting, fleecy masses of greenish-white blossoms that persist through the summer. Neither insects nor disease plague it.

Flowers/Fruit: Abundant, greenish-white flower, ½″ long, carried on 6″–8″ long panicles. Blooming begins in June and continues until September.

Foliage: Mature leaves are alternate, lanceolate, and entire, 1″–1½″ long, shiny bright green. New foliage emerges light green and blushed with red at the tips. Foliage is secondary and, in fact, the plant is ungainly in habit. Without its glorious flowers, the vine has nothing to recommend it.

Height/Habit: To 25′. Twining climber with wiry, intertwining stems.

Culture: Very accommodating, thriving in sunny situations with average moisture, but tolerant of a wide range of soil compositions, aridity, and wind. Winterkills, but this vine recovers eagerly in early spring, sending up dozens of vigorous new shoots.

Uses: Ideal for festooning porches, pergolas, arbors and—with adequate support on which to twine—walls and fences. An impressive accent plant for close-in views when in bloom.

Propagation: Seed, vegetative propagation of branches, and by division. Mature seeds germinate quickly in moist soil. Branch cuttings of half-ripe wood should be rooted in moist sand, vermiculite, and milled peat moss. After two or three seasons, the plant may be divided as one would overgrown perennials.

Pruning: To prevent legginess, nip out tips during the summer. Prune back hard to live wood and thin each year, in fall.

A related species, the Bokara Vine (*P. baldschua-nicum*), is almost as choice, with more restrained growth (to about 20'), flowers that turn pinkish to rose with age, and heart-shaped instead of lanceolate leaves.

Tripterygium regelii, Three-Wing Nut (5+) Although it is frequently difficult to find, this charming plant, which is technically a semi-climbing shrub with sprawling tendencies, rather than a classic vine, is well worth the quest. Its appealing characteristics make it a valuable addition as an accent in the home garden. It has dense, interesting, deciduous foliage, abundant flowers and decorative fruits, is easy of culture, and is not bothered by pests or disease.

Flowers/Fruit: Greenish-white flowers ¼" in diameter are borne in large, terminal panicles in summer, usually beginning in early July. These are followed by one-seeded, three-winged samaras ¾" long, in fall.

Foliage: Leaves are alternate, broadly elliptic, toothed, 3"–6" long, and are carried on reddish-brown stems.

Height/Habit: To 30', although 15'–20' is average. Semi-climbing or sprawling shrub.

Culture: Best specimens are grown in sunny situations in fertile, moist, well-drained soil. However, the plant will thrive in a broad spectrum of soil compositions with adequate moisture and good drainage. Tolerates heat, cold, wind, and a variety of coastal conditions. Needs a sturdy support. Tie and guide stems to direct plant upwards.

Uses: Accent and excellent plant for temporary screens.

Propagation: Seed and hardwood cuttings. New growth starts from base, so lower leaves should be left on cuttings. (See Chapter 10 for technique for rooting hardwood cuttings.)

Pruning: If needed, prune and shape plant in early spring.

Two related species are also deserving of attention. *T. forrestii* has lustrous green leaves and greenish-white flowers similar to those of *T. regelii*, but with purplish-red anthers. Not as hardy as the former, but equally vigorous, reaching up to 40' after a few seasons under ideal conditions. *T. wilfordii*, called the Thundergod Vine in China, is more dedicated to climbing than *T. regelii*, achieving heights of 35' or more. Foliage is nearly the same as the former, but its fruit is purplish-red to brown. Decoctions of its foliage have long been used as a natural insecticide in China.

Vitis coignetiae, Crimson Glory Vine (5) A Japanese native, Crimson Glory Vine is the best of the *Vitis* species, with inedible fruit and decorative applications in the home garden. It is a lush, vigorous vine with thick, ropy stems that makes a bold foliage display from summer to fall. Because it is deciduous, it is best confined to locations away from the house.

Flowers/Fruit: Insignificant flowers in panicles are produced in summer. Inedible black fruits ⅓" in diameter follow blooming, in fall.

Foliage: The large, heart-shaped leaves are the *raison d'être* for collecting this vine. They are alternative, slightly toothed, rich green with a rose blush above, and about 10" long. They clothe stems in a massed-effect. With the first cool weather, leaves put on a fiery display of scarlets and crimsons and cling well into the late fall.

Height/Habit: To 60'. Tendril climber.

Culture: An undemanding and forgiving plant. While it prefers a sunny situation and fertile, moist, well-drained soil, it grows with equal abandon in partial shade, a broad mix of soil types, and tolerates heat, cold, coastal conditions, and some wind. Because of its immense bulk, it requires a strong support. Young stems should be guided in the desired direction.

Uses: Accent, specimen, temporary screen, and as a covering for deep shade on arbors and pergolas.

Propagation: Mound layering gives quick results. Cover a portion of a trailing branch with soil. When rooting occurs, remove and pot to hold for fall or spring planting.

Pruning: Rampant growth can be curtailed for the following season by hard pruning in fall or early spring. Also, take out dead wood when seen.

Wisteria sinensis, Chinese Wisteria (5) This is the species most often planted in American gardens, favored because its blooms all open simultaneously for an impressive, long-lasting floral show. It is, without a doubt, the most popular flowering vine in the U.S., with one of the broadest ranges of any.

Flowers/Fruit: Pea-shaped, lightly fragrant, violet-blue flowers are produced in compact, pendant clusters, 6″–14″ long, as early as April, just before leaves appear. Unfortunately, most plants do not bloom for several seasons since they require a number of years to build a store of food before transferring energy to

Wisteria sinensis, **Chinese Wisteria**

HARDY VINES

floral production. Fruit is a flat, staked seed pod.
Foliage: Compound. Seven to 13 fernlike leaflets, each 2″–3″ long, make up each leaf.
Height/Habit: To 40′. Twining climber.
Culture: Wisterias perform best in sunny locations in a moist, well-drained, humusy medium. They require large volumes of water when in bloom. Once established, they will tolerate shade for part of the day. Add superphosphate in the fall or early spring to spur abundant flowering.

New plants are often difficult to establish and are prone to suffer transplant shock. The safest method for handling transplants is to plant the vine in its container after first carefully removing the bottom of the can or tub. This avoids disturbing the roots unduly.

First, excavate a hole three times as wide as the container and twice as deep. If the native soil is fertile and well-draining, no amendments need to be added to the backfill. But if the soil is clayey or overly sandy, mix one shovelful of compost to every two of native soil and add this to the planting hole beneath and around the container.

To train vines on trellises or wires, select three healthy shoots to guide up each wire. Keeping the stems from twining around each other prevents constriction, which can lead to dieback. To achieve a handsome tree form, stake juvenile plants and prune off all the shoots except the one that will be brought on as the trunk. Nip out any branch buds until the shoot reaches the desired height, then let it branch. Head back the shoot to three eyes in early spring for four or five seasons to promote a thick, sturdy trunk that needs no staking. Admittedly, creating a tree form is a long process, but the result is well worth the wait.
Uses: Stunning on arbors, pergolas, porches, against walls on wire grids and as a dwarf weeping tree.

Propagation: Cuttings and layers. Cuttings taken in late summer can be rooted in moist sand, vermiculite, and milled peat moss. Layers are usually successful but take several months.
Pruning: Immature vines need only their growing tips pinched the first five or six years to transfer energy, strengthening the stems. Mature vines are routinely pruned just after flowers fade. Branches are headed back to about five buds above the crown. Since Wisteria blooms are produced on spurs, this technique enhances the prospect of a productive flowering season the following spring. Old, weak vines that have begun to bloom sparsely are usually root-pruned to rejuvenate them. This also curbs excessive foliage growth, but is a process better left to an expert.

There are three outstanding cultivars available: *W. s.* 'Alba', the only white-flowered Chinese wisteria. Its highly fragrant blooms appear in April or May, depending on where it is grown; *W. s.* 'Purpurea', the pale purple-flowered form that is seen everywhere; and *W. s.* 'Plena', a double-flowered form.

A hardier species than *W. sinensis*, gaining more devotees each year, is Japanese Wisteria (*W. floribunda*), which prospers as far north as southern Canada. It has long been considered something of a stepchild because of its blooming habits. Flowering begins at the base of each cluster and progresses to the pendant tip. When the blooms at the tip open, those at the base have faded, detracting considerably from the vine's appearance. There are several varieties available, all with very fragrant flowers. The best of these are *W. f.* 'Alba' (white flowers); *W. f.* 'Issai' (violet-blue blooms); and *W. f.* 'Rosea' (pink flowers). Japanese Wisteria can be identified by its foliage. Its leaves are compound, composed of 13–19 leaflets, while Chinese Wisteria leaves have 7–13.

Wisteria floribunda **'Longissima Alba'**, Japanese Wisteria

4

Annual Climbers

***Lathyrus odoratus*, Sweet Pea**

Vines that are classified as annuals are frost-tender plants, usually with herbaceous stems and planted from seed, that live for one season, bloom, set seed, then die and must be started anew each spring. Some seed-bearing annuals, such as Morning Glory (*Ipomoea* sp.), self-sow in place and regenerate themselves.

Other annuals, grown in mild-winter areas, survive through winter and act like perennials. Still others, grown in northern and eastern gardens, may be taken up, potted, and brought into a warm indoor location or greenhouse and carried through the cold-weather months. This technique is sometimes practised when frost-tender perennials are grown in areas beyond their northern zonal limitation, but these plants are more often treated as annuals in these regions and are restarted each spring.

While in most cases annual vines don't have the permanence of perennial herbaceous and woody types, they are valuable additions to the garden. They offer quick, seasonal coverage of fences, posts, chain-link fences (which always need camouflaging), and outbuildings, and—with Sweet Pea (*Lathyrus odoratus*) and Nasturtium(*Tropaeolum* sp.)—serve as a source of cut flowers for the home. With Morning Glories grown in the north and east, vines bring a fresh splash of color to a garden in late summer to fall when other flowering species have begun to fade.

Most annual vines are twining climbers that quickly scamper up strings, wires, and posts or, if left to their own devices, wend their way up, through, and over other vegetation, festooning it with delightful chains of color and foliage. In general, they are undemanding vines that need little in the way of fussing over. While most plants perform best in rich garden loam, many annuals (such as Nasturtium and Morning Glory) are more productive in lean, unimproved media where only weeds can prosper.

Finally, because of their brief life, modest demands, and floral and foliage beauty, a number of annual vines are ideal choices for seasonal container culture as accent plants in pots, boxes, and hanging baskets close to the house.

The letter code that appears in parentheses after each vine's common name identifies the type of plant it is. A = Annual; HA = Hardy Annual; HP = Hardy Perennial; HHP = Half Hardy Perennial; and TP = Tender Perennial.

Asarina antirrhinifolia (also known as *A. antirrhinum*), Chickabiddy, Climbing Snapdragon (TP)
This is the best known of a group of tender perennial

climbers related to Snapdragons (*Antirrhinum* sp.) that bear trumpet-shaped flowers. They are refined vines, reaching an average of only 10′, and are useful as quick-response accent climbers, especially in small gardens where more rampant plants are inappropriate.

Flowers/Fruit: Blooms are rose-pink to reddish-purple, about 2″ long, funnelform, appearing as early as June.

Foliage: Leaves are heart-shaped, toothed, from 1″–2″ long, reminiscent of English Ivy (*Hedera helix*).

Height/Habit: To 10′. Twining climber.

Culture: Prefers moist, fertile soil and sunny situations. Tolerant of a variety of soil compositions and partial shade.

Uses: On light trellises against walls, porch railings, and in containers.

Propagation: Seed and cuttings. Vines started from seed in late winter or early spring flower in summer. Cuttings may be taken after Christmas and rooted in moist vermiculite and sand.

Pruning: Seldom needed. Pinching out growing tips encourages bushiness.

A. barclaiana bears flowers that open pink and gradually change to deep purple. Leaves are ¾″ long and hastate. Vine reaches an average of 10′ in height. *A. erubescens*, Creeping Gloxinia, has flowers that are 2″–3″ long with a rose-pink corolla and lobes that are notched. Leaves are shiny, 1½″–3″ long, deltoid, and toothed. Average height is 6′. Some plants sold as *A. scandens* are actually *A. erubescens*.

Bryonopsis laciniosa (also known as *Diplocyclos palmatus*), Bryonia (TP)

Another of the tender perennials that are grown as annuals. It produces climbing, tendril-bearing stems from tubers planted in spring and blooms by summer.

Flowers/Fruit: In summer, bears yellow, monoecious (bisexual) flowers that are often hidden under foliage. Fruit is a berry, ¾″ in diameter, that is first green with white stripes, reminiscent of a minute watermelon, then turns bright red as it ripens. These contain the seed of the species.

Foliage: Similar to that of ivy, but with deeper cuts in 3–5 lobes. Leaves have a rough surface and are an attractive light green.

Height/Habit: To 12′. Twining climber.

Culture: Prospers in humusy soil with average moisture and full sun. Takes off in hot, humid locations. Before first freeze, dig and clean tubers and store them in a cool, dry spot, as one would tender bulbs.

Uses: Outstanding fence and arbor cover. Good greenhouse plant.

Propagation: Seed and division of tubers. Sow seed in peat pots in late winter or very early spring and set out after frost danger has passed, or after soil warms sow in place outdoors. Stored tubers may be divided and planted in spring.

Pruning: Seldom needed.

Calonyction aculeatum (also known as *Ipomoea alba* and *Ipomoea bona-nox*), Moonflower (TP)

Commonly sold as a Morning Glory, Moonflower is a tender, perennial tropical vine that does not like frost or excessive cold. It is a vigorous plant that produces several twining, wirelike stems and offshoots clothed with dense foliage and large, white, saucerlike blooms that open in the evening to release their heady fragrance. Sometimes troubled by aphids, which can be controlled with insecticidal soap or rotenone-based organic insecticides.

Flowers/Fruit: Among the largest flowers produced by any of the vining plants, the satiny white, 5″–6″ wide salverform blossoms, sometimes accented with green, unfurl in early evening or on overcast days beginning in July and continuing to bloom until the first frost.

Foliage: Soft green, heart-shaped, alternate leaves, 3″–8″ long, are densely set on stems.

Height/Habit: Well-grown vines may reach 40′. Twining climber.

Culture: Best plants are grown in a moist, well-drained, humusy medium and full-sun location. Intolerant of frost, which kills it to the ground.

Uses: As a seasonal screen, covering for shade on arbors and pergolas, as an accent in a white (or night) garden, and on porches and posts near the house where its beauty and perfume may be enjoyed.

Propagation: Seed and cuttings. Commercially propagated from cuttings, but plants grow rapidly from properly prepared seed. Hard seed coatings must be scarified or softened by overnight soaking in warm water, or germination will be slow and percentage reduced. Vines propagated from collected seed come true to species.

Pruning: Seldom needed. Pinch tips to control rampant growth, if desired.

Calonyction aculeatum, **Moonflower**

Cobaea scandens, Coral Bells, Cup-and-Saucer Vine (TP)   A tropical, tender perennial from Mexico, this handsome, prolific bloomer is named to honor Father Cobo, a 17th-century Spanish naturalist and Jesuit missionary. It is a rapid grower, treated as a perennial in mild-winter climates and as an annual in other areas where it is started anew from seed each spring.

Flowers/Fruit: Blooms emerge on stalks from leaf axils and change from greenish-white buds to violet or deep purple flowers, although those of the cultivar 'Alba' remain a pure white. The five-lobed corolla is bell-shaped, about 2″ long and ½″–1½″ wide with protruding stamens. Corollas are set on a saucerlike calyx, which is the source of the vine's popular common name. Flowering spans midsummer to frost. Insignificant fruits, somewhat plumlike in appearance, follow blooms in the fall.

Foliage: Dull green leaves are alternate and compound, composed of 4–6 oval or oblong 4″ leaflets. The terminal leaf produces a branched tendril.

Height/Habit: Quickly reaches 25′ or more. Tendril climber.

Culture: Prefers warmth, but needs some protection from the sun in torrid summer areas. Likes moist, well-drained, fertile soil. Tolerant of less-than-ideal conditions, but suffers from wind-whipping and dies back in cold weather.

Uses: As a seasonal screen and for arbor and pergola covers for shade. In hot-summer areas, train on support against an east- or south-facing wall.

Propagation: Seed. Start seeds two months before last frost in moist vermiculite and light potting soil. Set the seeds on edge and push them into the germination medium leaving only the top edge exposed. Seeds planted flat often rot. When frost danger has passed and seedlings have developed two true leaves, set them out in fertile loam that is kept evenly moist.

Pruning: Nip out growing tips of young plants to keep stems bushy. If needed, and where vine is grown as a perennial, prune to train and control.

Dolichos lablab, **Hyacinth Bean**

Dolichos lablab, Hyacinth Bean (TP)   This tropical native, a perennial that must be treated as an annual in the U.S. in all but the warm, humid South and the Sunbelt because of its intolerance of cold, is a fast, abundantly flowering vine with lush foliage that climbs by twining stems. Largely resistant to pests and disease.

Flowers/Fruit: From midsummer to frost, the vine is resplendent with masses of pure white or purple, pea-shaped, 1″ long blooms that have a light, pleasant fragrance. Blooms are profuse and carried on stiff 6″–8″ long stems well above the foliage. They are long-lived cut flowers. When flowers fade, decorative flat purplish seed pods 2″–2½″ long appear. These contain the seeds of the species and may be either white or black.

Foliage: Equally attractive are the light green, heart-shaped leaves that are alternate and compound, with three oval leaflets, 3″–6″ long.

Height/Habit: To 25′, under ideal conditions. Twining climber.

Culture: Best vines are usually seen in the steamy southern U.S., where the plant's preference for heat and humidity is met. Plant in the sun in a light, humusy, well-drained soil that is kept evenly moist. Will tolerate cool conditions but not frosts, which kill it to the ground.

Uses: So long as it is provided with the proper support for its twining stems to coil around, it can be used in any garden location where its foliage mass can be utilized and its flowers appreciated.

Propagation: Seed. Start indoors in March for seedlings that can be set out in May, or sow in place at this time. Since seedlings are difficult to transplant successfully because they are susceptible to shock if roots are disturbed, sow in peat pots that can be dropped into the planting hole.

Pruning: Seldom needed. Growing tips may be pinched periodically to control rampant growth, if needed.

A similar variety that prospers in U.S. Zone 10 is Australian Pea, *D. lignosis,* which is also a dense perennial with evergreen foliage and clusters of white or pinkish-purple flowers. Two cultivars occasionally seen in gardens and catalogs are 'Enormis' and 'Giganteus'.

Eccremocarpus scaber, Chilean Glory Flower, Chilean Glory Vine (HP) While this colorful vine is classified as a hardy perennial, it will not survive winters where freezes are the norm and must be treated as an annual. It is one of the easiest vines to grow from seed and one of the quickest to flower. Modern hybrids have produced a wide range of floral hues, including bicolors. Largely pest- and disease-free.

Flowers/Fruit: Bears clusters of tubular flowers 1¼″ long that flare at the mouth, mostly in yellows, oranges, and reds. Blooming continues into fall. Fruits are seed capsules 1½″ long, produced in fall, that have no decorative value.

Foliage: Leaves are a lustrous bright green, opposite and twice compound, with oval leaflets ½″–1″ long.

Height/Habit: To 12′. Tendril climber.

Culture: An eminently adaptable vine that prefers warmth and even moisture, but one that will tolerate a broad range of conditions, with the exception of prolonged cold. Thrives in fertile, sandy media that is frequently irrigated in hot weather. When grown as a perennial in areas where winters are occasionally frigid, provide some protection for roots. Treat as an annual in northern and eastern U.S. gardens.

Uses: Accent, seasonal screen, arbor, trellis, and pergola cover. Twines efficiently on wire grids.

Propagation: Seed. Since seedlings do not transplant well, sow seeds two months before the last seasonal frost in peat pots that can be set out when climatically safe. Seeds may also be sown in place as soon as the soil begins to warm.

Pruning: Seldom needed. When grown as a perennial, head plant back to a few inches above ground in late fall or early spring to rejuvenate.

Echinocystis lobata, Wild Cucumber, Wild Balsam Apple (A) Called mock cucumber or wild cucumber because of its prickly seed pods, this annual vine grows like a weed and is considered one in many regions because of its rampant growth and self-sowing habit. It is an excellent cover for camouflaging unsightly objects in the yard.

Flowers/Fruit: Lovely small white flowers, massed in branched sprays above the foliage, are produced from summer to frost. Fruits are somewhat decorative seed pods, about 2″ long, bristling with spines and having the appearance of small cucumbers. These follow the blooming cycle in fall.

Foliage: Leaves are alternate, 3″–5″ long and nearly as broad, with five lobes.

Height/Habit: To 30′. Tendril climber.

Culture: Plant's needs are furnished by nature. It is a hardscrabble vine that fends for itself.

Uses: Temporary cover for eyesores. Takes readily to chainlink fences.

Propagation: Seed. Sow seeds in place in October or November for earliest start. Spring-sown seeds should be soaked overnight in warm water to soften seed covering. Plant often proliferates by self-sowing.

Pruning: Common practice is to remove plants entirely in the fall, after they die back.

***Luffa aegyptiaca,* Chinese Luffa Sponge**

Gourds (various species)   A variety of plant types are grouped under this appellation, *Benincasa, Cucumis, Cucurbita, Lagenaria,* and *Luffa* being the most popular for home culture. Treated as annuals, they range from herbaceous types to massive, woody vines. Grown as garden curiosities by modern gardeners, gourds have been cultivated for centuries for their utilitarian applications as utensils and for their decorative beauty. A resurgence of interest in growing certain kinds of gourds for crafts, such as birdhouse-making, has developed.

Flowers/Fruit: Blooms are usually bold, bell-shaped, bright yellow, and typical of familiar *Cucurbita* flowers. Fruits are variously shaped. The common name is an indication of the form—apple, bottle, calabash, dipper, egg, gooseberry, Hercules Club, orange, pear, and serpent. Colors include white, yellow, orange, green, as well as striped and mottled bicolors.

Another popular type, which produces fruits that resemble a large, smooth cucumber, is the *Luffa cylindrica,* commonly called the Luffa Sponge, Dishcloth Gourd, and Towel Gourd. When it is harvested and dried, its skin may be peeled back and the fibre inside can be dried to produce a durable bath sponge.

Lagenarias (bottle, calabash, dipper, serpent, and spoon) should not be harvested until their shells have hardened. In the north, this is usually after frost has killed the vine. Remove the gourds from the vine with as much stem as possible and dry them in a cellar or garage for 10–14 days. Gourds that will be lacquered should be soaked overnight in a tub of warm water to soften protective coating. After soaking, this outer "skin" can be removed with a soft-bristled brush or a piece of burlap. Return the gourds to their drying site for another week. After this final curing period, they are ready to be lacquered or waxed.

Foliage: Leaves are mostly bold, toothed, lobed, or heart-shaped, depending on species, often downy or hairy, ranging in color from bright green to grey-green, and some are splotched yellow or white.

Height/Habit: From 20'–40', depending on species. Tendril climbers.

Culture: Full sun and fertile, humusy soil, kept evenly moist, produce the most vigorous vines and best-looking fruits. In areas where cutworms are a problem, use protective collars pressed three or four inches into the soil around seedlings. To avoid mildew and other fungal diseases, don't wet foliage when irrigating, especially late in the day. If mildew appears, dust plants with sulfur.

Uses: On trellises and fences and, if allowed to run, on slopes and banks. Less rampant, daintier types may be used on verandas and porch railings. Match support structure to the bulk of the vine.

Propagation: Seed. Start seeds indoors in March for setting out seedlings after frost danger has passed. Mid- to late April is the time for direct sowing, except for frost-free areas, where seeds may be sown in place as early as February.

Pruning: Prune to control rambunctious growth and to redirect vine's energy into producing and nurturing fruits, rather than foliage.

Humulus japonicus, Hop Vine, Japanese Hop Vine (A)   Another vine "in a hurry," the Hop Vine will quickly cover an arbor with a thick blanket of foliage by midsummer. Like Kiwis (*Actinidia deliciosa*), there are male and female vines, and only the female, which is more delicate and produces slightly smaller leaves, bears "hops," which are only marginally of decorative value. Thus, both sexes must be planted.
Flowers/Fruit: Male plants produce greenish flowers in pendent panicles from 5″–10″ long. Females bear paired floral spikes under a narrow bract. Both sexes bloom in early to mid-summer. Fruits are so-called hops, the mature form of the female flower, but not the true hop of commerce.
Foliage: Large, handsome, bright green leaves, 6″–8″ wide with 5–7 deeply cut lobes that form an overlapping blanket of foliage. The variety *variegatus* has leaves that are marbled or accented white.
Height/Habit: To 35′. Twining climber.
Culture: Does best in hot summers and fertile, evenly moist soil, in sun or partial shade. Once established, it is fairly drought tolerant.
Uses: As a seasonal screen and as a source of deep shade when grown on arbors, pergolas, and porches. Makes a decorative wall screen when trained on a trellis.
Propagation: Seed. For an early start, sow seeds in place in the fall or early spring. Seed sown after weather warms often remains dormant until the following spring. Plant is a rampant self-sower.
Pruning: Seldom needed.

Ipomoea purpurea (also sold as *I. nil*), Morning Glory (A)   Largely because of their universality and propensity for producing numerous offspring, once they've been invited into the garden, Morning Glories don't always get the respect they deserve as hard-working, undemanding vines that will provide a quick, colorful accent wherever one is needed. Another of their frequently cited drawbacks—the fact

***Ipomoea* sp., Morning Glory**

that most bloom in late summer when everything else is winding down—is actually an asset. Morning Glories provide a welcome extension of the summer flowering season into fall, when other plants have long since gone to seed. One *can* get blooms weeks earlier by starting seed indoors a month before they can safely be sown in the garden.
Flowers/Fruit: Blooms are funnelform, 1″–3″ long, and run the color gamut from solid hues to shades of white, pink, crimson, purple, and blue. There are also double-flowering cultivars. Among the named varieties that have gained favor over the years are: 'Darling' (wine-red flowers with a white throat); 'Giant Cornell' (large carnelian red, bordered white); 'Pearly

Gates' (a large white); and the ever-popular 'Scarlett O'Hara' (rosy red). 'Heavenly Blue' is sometimes listed under *I. purpurea*. It is a variety of *I. tricolor*.
Foliage: Leaves are alternate, to 5″ long, heart-shaped, and a deep green.
Height/Habit: To 20′. Twining climber.
Culture: Prospers in sunny locations and well-drained, sandy loam, but will tolerate all but swampy soils and heavy clay.
Uses: Accent, seasonal screen, cover for arbors, pergolas, porches, posts, fences, and trellises. Ideal for camouflaging chainlink fences. Readily climbs wire and string. Most do well in containers equipped with a trellis or other appropriate support.
Propagation: Seed. In colder climes, start seeds in peat pots indoors six weeks before setting seedlings into the garden, which should be done after frost danger has passed. Sow in place in spring, after last frost. If seeds of Japanese Morning Glories are to be sown, soak them overnight in warm water or scarify them to promote faster germination.
Pruning: Seldom needed. If self-sowing is a problem, snip off spent blooms before they set seed.

Other useful species are:

Blue Moonflower, or Dawnflower (*I. leari*), a tender perennial that bears 4″ blooms that are a deep-violet with five bands of slightly lighter blue and with a white throat. Flowers first open in late July or early August and continue until the first frost. It attains 35′ of height.

Brazilian Morning Glory (*I. setosa*), distinguished by its three-lobed, grapelike leaves up to 10″ across, and by the purple down on its stems. Also a tender perennial, it bears an abundance of rosy-purple flowers about mid- to late August and reaches 30′.

Horsfall Morning Glory (*I. horsfalliae briggsi*), a tender perennial, may not perform well except in the warmth and humidity of Zone 10 but it is worth a try elsewhere. It is a spectacular bloomer, producing two

seasons of flowers—in winter, usually around December, and again in early summer. The beautiful crimson-magenta blossoms are 2½″ long. Its foliage, almost as handsome, is glossy dark green and deeply cut. It grows to about 40′.

Japanese Morning Glory (*I. imperialis*) is a much-improved species developed in Japan. It produces larger flowers in a broader range of colors than any other. Leaves are deeply cut instead of heart-shaped. To 20′.

Cypress Vine (*Quamoclit pennata*) and Moon-flower (*Calonyction acculeatum*), described elsewhere in the book, are technically classified as *Ipomoeas*.

Lathyrus odoratus, Sweet Pea (HA) Sweet Peas are among the oldest plants in cultivation. Their fragrance and delicate blooms have captivated gardeners since ancient times. They have been much improved over the years by breeders who have produced heat-resistant strains and varieties with large flowers in a dazzling array of colors. Their reputation for being difficult plants is undeserved and springs from inexperienced gardeners attempting to grow them without preparing the growing site properly.
Flowers/Fruit: Blooms are nearly identical to those of the garden pea, but are variously colored from white to yellow and red through blue, and up to 2″ wide. They appear separately or grouped on branched stalks in great abundance. Fruits are 2″ long hairy pods.
Early Flowering Types. Formerly called Early Spencers, the correct designation now is Early Flowering Multifloras or Early Multifloras. These are for mild-winter regions and will bloom in midwinter in these areas. They are available in mixed colors and are not heat-tolerant. To produce plants that bloom by the end of December, seeds should be started in late summer.
Spring Flowering Types. These are referred to as Heat-Resistant Cuthbertson types, Cuthbertson Floribundas, and Zvolanek Strain Floribundas. They are

available in mixed hues as well as in single colors and have a broad color range, including white, creamy white, salmon, pink, rose, scarlet red, and blue. Seed of these varieties should be sown in cold-winter areas in late fall and, in mild-winter regions, very early in the spring, provided the soil is not overly wet.

Summer Flowering Types. These are the Galaxy and Plenti-Flora heat-resistant Sweet Peas. Several named varieties are offered, as well as mixes, and they have a fairly wide color range. In harsh-winter areas, sow seeds in late fall, before the first hard freeze. In mild-winter zones, spring planting is the norm.

Foliage: Compound leaves 1″–2″ long and mostly oval. Some leaves are tendril-bearers.

Height/Habit: To 7′. Tendril climber.

Culture: Generally, Sweet Peas prefer sun and deeply cultivated, cool, humusy, well-drained soil that is kept evenly moist. They deteriorate when the sun bakes the ground where they are growing. Varieties are available that prosper in specific geographical areas (see above). Vines will often stop budding unless blooms are picked frequently, usually every other day. They are decorative, long-lived cut flowers.

Proper preparation of the planting site is essential to healthy, productive vines and large blooms. In the fall, while the ground is still workable, prepare a trench that is a foot deep (18″, if soil is lean or clayey). Mix one part well-rotted manure to two parts backfill soil and blend in a complete organic fertilizer, in volume recommended on the package. Return this amended soil to the trench to a depth of six inches. Then, fill the trench with unimproved native soil, if fertile, or soil amended with well-ground compost. Hill up the soil so that it is three or four inches above grade. Install light trellis structures, strings, wires, or netting. Sow seeds one inch deep and cover the area with a 3″–4″ deep layer of compost.

Uses: Accent, quick seasonal cover, and as a source of cut flowers.

Propagation: Seed. In areas where spring planting is recommended, ensure efficient germination and gain a three- or four-week head start by sowing seeds in-

Lathyrus odoratus, **Sweet Pea**

doors, in March, in peat pots filled with moist vermiculite and milled peat moss. First, soak seeds overnight in warm water to soften the seed covers, then dry and dust with a fungicide. Drop three seeds per pot 1″ deep and cover with plastic wrap that has several holes punched in its surface to evacuate excess moisture condensation and prevent mildew. Remove plastic when seedlings appear. When soil in the garden is workable, transplant pots of seedlings outdoors in hilled-up soil for good drainage and pinch out growing tips to promote branching. Wait to thin seedlings to one every six inches until you are certain they are all viable. Keep plants well watered, especially while they are getting established.

Pruning: Periodic pinching of the growing tips promotes branching. Spent blossoms should be removed to spur greater floral production.

Maurandia barclaiana (also sold as *Asarina barclaiana*), Maurandia (TP) Profuse blooming from spring until frost, and restrained, well-mannered growth, make this tender perennial from Mexico a favorite for close-by-the-house applications. It will

***Lathyrus latifolius,* Perennial Sweet Pea**

happily twine its way up string or wire, or cascade delightfully over the edges of porch and windowboxes, blooming early the first year from seed. Occasionally plagued by aphids and red spider mites. The former may be discouraged by frequent light misting; the latter can be eradicated with insecticidal soap.

Flowers/Fruit: Abundant, trumpetlike blooms are produced in leaf axils. Flowers are 1½″–3″ long with a pinkish corolla that changes to deep purple with age. There are varieties with other colors, mostly shades of white and rose-purple.

Foliage: Leaves are bright green, ¾″ long, angularly lobed, borne on twining petioles.

Height/Habit: To 10′. Twining climber.

Culture: Ideal growing conditions are sun to partial shade and humusy, moist, well-drained soil. Vine suffers in hot and cold extremes. Where it is grown as an annual, remove spent plants in the fall and start with new seedlings in early spring. In mild-winter areas, vine will come back with renewed vigor in early spring. Plant benefits from monthly feedings through the summer of a balanced, soluble organic fertilizer.

Uses: Since Maurandias trail as well as climb and are rather shallow-rooted, they can be used as pot plants in containers equipped with wire, string, or a light trellis, and as porch or windowbox accents.

Propagation: Seed and cuttings. Seeds germinate readily without special techniques in moist sand, vermiculite, and milled peat moss. Start seeds indoors in February and move seedlings up to larger pots when two true leaves have formed. In cold-winter regions, set out seedlings or sow seeds in place in early May. Cuttings taken in midsummer may be rooted in moist sand and vermiculite. Dip cut ends in a rooting hormone before inserting in rooting medium.

Pruning: None required.

Momordica balsamina, Balsam Apple (A) Primarily grown for its odd, decorative fruit, this annual climber makes an interesting novelty plant, and its handsome foliage alone is sufficiently ornamental to recommend the vine. Fruit set is sparse in all but hot, humid climates. It is occasionally threatened by cutworms, snails, and both chewing and sucking insects. Organic controls for these pests can be found in Chapter 9.

Flowers/Fruit: Largely inconspicuous, creamy-white, or pale yellow blooms, sometimes accented with brown, about 1″ wide, are produced in summer. Male and female flowers are separate on the same plant. Orangish oval fruits resembling apples appear in the fall. The capsules are 3″ long and split open late in the season to display rows of bright scarlet seeds.

Foliage: Leaves have deep lobes, sharp teeth, are thin, glossy, and from 1″–4″ broad.

Height/Habit: To 20′. Tendril climber.

Culture: Thrives in warm, humid conditions in a light, moist soil rich in humus. Deteriorates in cold or dry environments.

Uses: Accent vine on trellises or wire grids. Good on open fences and as a stump cover.

Propagation: Seeds sown indoors in March in a moist mix of sand, vermiculite, and milled peat moss germinate readily. Set seedlings out or sow seed in place in early May in harsh-winter regions.

Pruning: None needed.

An equally popular, very similar species is Balsam Pear (*M. charantia*). Its tiny yellow flowers appear along its stems in early summer. Pear-shaped, yellowish-orange warty fruits, 1″–8″ long, develop in the fall and, like Balsam Apple's, burst when ripe to reveal neat rows of colorful red arils.

***Phaseolus coccineus,* Scarlet Runner Bean**

Phaseolus coccineus, (also known as *P. mutliflorus*), Scarlet Runner Bean (TP) One of the best of the red-flowering vines, Scarlet Runner Bean blooms profusely and continuously throughout the summer months, then produces decorative fruits, which are edible peas.

Flowers/Fruit: Racemes of rich scarlet pea-shaped blooms, 1″ long, in clusters of 10–30 flowers, cover the vine all summer. Fruits are flat pods 4″–12″ long that are first green, then purple at maturity. They contain the seeds of the species, which are a striking black, mottled red. The beans are often harvested and eaten while the pods are still green.

Foliage: Leaves are alternate and compound with three light green broadly ovate leaflets about 3″ wide.

Height/Habit: To 20′. Twining climber.

Culture: Prospers in full sun and moist, fertile media. Cultivate planting site deeply and work in leaf mold and well-rotted manure. Tolerates warm coastal conditions, but suffers in cold situations. Grown as an annual in all but mild-winter climates. Needs training at the outset to direct growth.

Uses: As an accent on porches and at entries, as a seasonal screen, and as a fence, trellis, and arbor cover.

Propagation: Seed, which may be started in March for setting out in the garden in May or sown directly in May. Planting media should be only barely moist and kept that way until germination. Seeds often rot in boggy soil. Drop seeds 2″ deep, 10″ apart in the garden.

Pruning: Seldom needed.

A cultivar very similar to Scarlet Runner Bean is the Dutch Case-Knife Bean (*P. c.* 'Albus'), which bears white flowers. Snailvine (*Vigna caracalla*, also sold as *Phaseolus caracalla*) is another frost-tender perennial species widely grown in warm winter portions of California and Florida, although it may be treated as an annual in less benign climates. It bears lightly scented, creamy-white flowers marked lavender-purple. The keel petals are coiled and are reminiscent of a snail shell. Both of the above have nearly the same culture requirements as Scarlet Runner Bean.

Quamoclit pennata, Cypress Vine (4) Prized for its delicate, fernlike foliage and star-shaped scarlet flowers that stand out in contrast against the dark green leaves. It is best grown against walls where the charm of its design tracery can be displayed to good effect. Unlike most flowers that bask in the sun, those of the Cypress Vine recoil from direct solar rays, only expanding completely after sundown and in the early morning hours. Untroubled by pests or disease.

Flowers/Fruit: Funnelform blooms are somewhat star-shaped, 1½″ long and—although scarlet is the most familiar floral color—some varieties produce white and orange flowers.

Foliage: Leaves are alternate and pinnately cut in threadlike segments similar to some of the delicate fern species. They are unusually dark green.

Height/Habit: To 20′. Twining climber.

Culture: Prospers in warmth and sun and in a light, humusy soil that is kept slightly moist. Tolerates shade and the more temperate coastal locations.

Quamoclit pennata, **Cypress Vine; Cardinal Climber**

Uses: Spectacular against walls where the tracery of its foliage can be appreciated. Also, an excellent accent for a small garden. Climbs strings and wires readily, but needs some initial guidance to direct growth.

Propagation: Seed. Hard seed cover needs scarifying, or soak seeds in warm water until they begin to swell. Start indoors in peat pots in March for seedlings that can be set out in May, or sow in place after frost danger has passed. Cover with ½″ of germinating media and keep the mix just barely moist. Plant self-sows if seeds are allowed to mature.

Pruning: None needed.

Two related species have similar characteristics. Scarlet Starglory (*Q. coccinea*) bears 1½″ scarlet flowers with a yellow throat, on stalks, from midsummer through October. Leaves are heart-shaped and 4″–6″ long. It reaches only about 10′ of height, but is more cold tolerant then *Q. pennata*. Cardinal Climber (*Q. sloteri*) is a hybrid resulting from a cross between *Q. coccinea* and *Q. pennata*. Its flowers are trumpet-shaped with a flaring mouth, cardinal-red with a white throat. Blooms are profuse with up to seven in a cluster. They open at dawn and close at sunset. Leaves are an attractive glossy green and forked. Under ideal conditions, grows to 15′ or more.

Thunbergia gregorii (also known as *T. gibsonii*), Orange Clockvine (TP)   A South African native, the Orange Clockvine is a tender perennial that is grown as an annual beyond U.S. Zone 9. Its intense orange flowers, produced in profusion, often clash with other colors in the garden, but it is a fine climber/trailer for making a bold statement wherever a vivid accent is needed.

Flowers/Fruit: Blooms are tubular, flaring, five-lobed, 1½″ broad, 1¾″ long, and a bright orange, borne singly on hairy stems. Flowers are copiously produced from early spring to fall in mild climates and through the hot summer months elsewhere.

Foliage: Leaves are heart-shaped, hirsute, and about 3″ long.

Height/Habit: To 20′, or covers about five feet when allowed to trail on the ground. Twining climber.

Culture: Thrives in full sun and evenly moist soil that has been improved with leaf mold or well-rotted manure.

Uses: Looks best on trellises and fences where there is no conflict with other nearby floral color. Suitable for container gardens, hanging baskets, and as a cover for banks and rocky terrain.

Propagation: Seed. In cold-winter regions, start seed indoors in peat pots in March. Set out seedlings in

***Thunbergia gregorii*, Orange Clockvine**

May, after frost danger has passed. Sow in place, fall or spring, in mild-winter areas.

Pruning: None required.

Equally popular, especially in the northern and eastern U.S., is the highly floriferous Black-Eyed Susan Vine (*T. alata*), a tender perennial that is hardier and more restrained, attaining only about 8′ feet of height. It also trails and is a good candidate for boxes, baskets, and containers. Flowers are similar to those of *T. gibsonii* in shape, but available colors include white, orange with a purple throat, and white with an

***Tropaeolum* sp., Nasturtium**

ebony throat. Leaves are somewhat triangular, coarsely toothed, 3″ long on petioles. Propagation is by seed or cuttings of young growth in very early spring.

Tropaeolum majus, Nasturtium (TP)   One of the few ornamentals that thrives on benign neglect, the climbing forms of Nasturtium are useful in many applications in the garden. They are fast from seed and, if felled by a late frost, can be quickly replaced by successive sowings. Immature flowers, leaves, and seed pods add a zest to fresh salads. Occasionally plagued by black aphids, which can be controlled by hosing or with insecticidal soap.

Flowers/Fruit: Blooms are lightly fragrant, 2″–3″ broad, and, depending on the variety, are single, semi-double, and double in form. Colors cover a broad range, including brown, cerise, cream, orange, scarlet, yellow, and bicolors.

Foliage: Leaves, attractive in their own right, are 3″–4″ across, light green, alternate, shield-shaped, and attached to a long petiole.

Height/Habit: To 8′. Twining climber/trailer.

Culture: Best plants are grown in sunny locations and lean, gravelly or sandy loam with indifferent irrigation. Soil that is too fertile prompts foliage growth at the expense of floral production.

Uses: Low fence covers, in windowboxes, hanging baskets, and other containers, and as a trailing ground-cover accent. Blooms are handsome, long-lasting cut flowers.

Propagation: Seed. Sow in place when the ground has begun to warm. May be started indoors in peat pots filled with moist sand and vermiculite. Germinates quickly.

Pruning: None required.

A popular related species is Canary Creeper, or Canary Bird Vine (*T. peregrinum*), which grows to about 10′. It bears masses of unusual fringed yellow flowers all summer that are reminiscent of canaries, hence the common name. Leaves are interesting, as well, with five deeply cut lobes and a light green color. Canary Creeper prospers in partial shade and fertile soil that is kept evenly moist through the summer.

ANNUAL CLIMBERS

5

Vines with Edible Fruit

Vines that bear edible fruit were undoubtedly the first plants collected and propagated by early humans. In an era when food was scarce and farming was a concept still centuries away from realization, the bounty of vine crops helped sustain our ancient roving ancestors. There is, of course, no record of how primitive people determined which fruits were edible and which were not, but it is probably safe to assume that, in their quest to fill their stomachs, a few of these adventurous souls gave their lives by ingesting some of the poisonous species whose descendants can still be found in feral areas.

Today, several species and improved cultivars of fruit-bearing vines provide, in addition to nourishment, decorative accents for a number of applications, including arbor and trellis covers, screens, and—for gardeners with little arable garden space—containers for close-in specimen accents.

Generally speaking, fruiting vines are no more difficult to grow than foliage or flowering types. The two notable exceptions are Kiwifruit (*Actinidia deliciosa*) and Grapes (*Vitis* sp.), both of which require complex pruning and intense training to bear crops in sufficient quantity to be worth the effort.

Actinidia deliciosa (also listed as *A. chinensis*), Kiwifruit, Chinese Gooseberry (8)

This odd, deciduous fruit vine was first introduced into the U.S. from Asia in the 1930s, but languished in anonymity until a few years ago. It wasn't until it was dubbed "Kiwifruit" and vigorously promoted that it caught the public's fancy.

Because it is still relatively new in commerce, its culture requirements are not definitely known. What *is* known is that only female vines bear fruit and, usually, only females are named varieties. A male vine, unceremoniously referred to as simply a "male kiwi," must be planted nearby to ensure efficient pollination of the female flowers. A single male vine will provide sufficient pollen to pollinate half a dozen or more females, but the average home gardener has room for only two or three.

Female flowers are largely scentless, creamy-white, aging to yellowish-orange, from 1"–1½" wide, and appear in May in mild-winter regions (but blooming may be a bit later in Zone 8). Blooms are followed by the curious, fuzzy fruits. Foliage is quite ornamental. Leaves are rounded to cordate at their base, to 7" long and nearly as broad. New leaves are covered with reddish hairs.

The most productive female cultivars bearing full-sized fruit are 'Chico', 'Hayward', and 'Vincent'. Cultivars that bear bumper crops of smaller fruit are 'Abbot', 'Bruno', and 'Monty'. All need a male pollinator. 'Blake', a new self-fruitful cultivar, produces slightly smaller fruits that ripen 2–3 weeks earlier than 'Hayward'.

Fruit/Harvesting: Egg-sized and shaped, from 3"–3½" long and about 2" in diameter, with a tan skin covered with soft fuzz. Clusters of fruit hang singly on stems 2"–3" long. These are harvested green in October or November and stored in a refrigerator, where they will keep for months. A few days before they are to be eaten, they are removed from refrigeration and allowed to ripen at room temperature. They are at their peak of ripeness when there is a slight "give" to them when lightly pressed between thumb and forefinger. When the peel is removed and the fruit is sliced open, the succulent, lime-green flesh is revealed. There are hundreds of tiny, edible black seeds arranged in a broad oval in the center of the fruit. The flavor is unique—a zesty medley of strawberry, gooseberry, and banana.

Culture: Most of the following information on the care of Kiwifruit vines is from Kathy Fives, owner of Northwoods Retail Nursery in Canby, Oregon, and one of the top experts on the species in the U.S. Northwoods is the source for the newest cultivar imports from Russia and New Zealand. Optimum growing conditions are a mild spring (no frosts or only light ones) and fall and a hot (90°F+) summer, but vines will thrive with less warmth. Male vines are not as hardy as females—15°F for males; 10°F for females—

Actinidia deliciosa, **Kiwifruit**

range of soil compositions, although a fertile, neutral to slightly acid (pH of 6–6.5) medium that drains well is ideal. Fruit will develop in partial shade, but volume is usually reduced. Chlorosis may appear in leaves on plants grown in overly alkaline soil. This can be corrected with a chelated iron foliar spray. Heavy clay should be improved and mounded where vines will be planted.

Vines need about 1½″ inches of water a week during the growing season. Deep watering once a week is better than two or three light spritzings. Nitrogen is important to the health of Kiwifruit, but Northwoods Retail Nursery counsels against feeding vines directly the first three years of growth. This advice is in conflict with that of some other experts, who recommend feeding begin the first year after planting. Mature (bearing) vines are given about 1½ pounds of actual nitrogen annually and younger plants should receive ¼ pound. This can be in the form of a complete fertilizer that contains other elements. Cut the volume in half and feed vines half in February and the remainder after fruit set on mature plants. Young plants should get the second half after growth begins in early spring.

In cold-winter climates, wrap the trunks of Kiwifruit vines with tree wrap to protect them against damage from weather and foraging rodents.

Propagation: Softwood cuttings. Although Kiwifruits can be propagated from seed, there is about a seven-year wait for resulting vines to bear. Vines propagated from softwood cuttings taken in June fruit much sooner. Northwoods' rooting medium is an equal mix of peat moss, perlite, and pumice. Place cuttings in a warm greenhouse or warm, bright indoor location.

Pruning: Correct pruning and training techniques are crucial to the production of bumper crops (each female vine can yield over 100 pounds of fruit) and maintenance of the plant. Kiwifruit vines are most productive when grown laterally on two T-bar trellises with sturdy cables or 12–14-gauge wires strung between them on which fruiting stems can be trained. The trellises should be about 6′ tall so that fruits,

but dormant vines of both sexes may survive lower temperatures. The real danger to the viability of *A. deliciosa* vines is a prolonged late spring frost, after tender new growth has emerged. Wind—especially a chilly one—tatters leaves and snaps vines, so plants should be sited out of the path of prevailing breezes.

As with many stone fruit bearers, *A. deliciosa* has a winter chill requirement (temperature below 45°F) of from 500–800 hours. This range is still inexact because of a lack of research data, but longer chilling periods seem to promote more prolific fruiting.

Kiwis prosper in sunny, protected sites in a broad

which hang on pendent stems, can be easily harvested from underneath. Young plants are set in under the trellis and secured to a temporary stake. All side shoots are pruned off at planting time and this procedure is continued until the vine reaches the support wires. When the main vine has grown 4″–5″ above the wires, nip the growing tip to 2″ below the wires to encourage branching. Choose two strong branches that result from heading the vine back to grow as permanent cordons and train these to twine in opposite directions on the wires. When they reach the T-bar trellis at each end, allow the stems to produce lateral branches. In early winter, prune these laterals to a point where there are six nodes. These will bear the fruits of next season's crop, since kiwis fruit on the current season's wood.

Canes that develop from these lateral branches will bear fruit near their bases. These are pruned back in June, leaving 5–10 buds beyond the last flower. Each winter, all canes that bore fruit, except for three, are removed. New fruiting wood will develop from these. Each cane bears fruit for about three years, then is pruned out and new fruiting canes are brought along.

Actinidia arguta, Hardy Kiwifruit, Tara Vine (4+)
This species of kiwi is popular in the northern and eastern U.S. because of its hardiness, surviving temperatures well below 0°F. Its fruit, only about a quarter the size of the so-called "fuzzy" kiwi, has a smooth, edible skin and ripens earlier—usually late summer. Flowers are slightly fragrant, white, about 1″ across. Leaves are broadly ovate, to 6″ long and sharply serrate.

Some of the most productive cultivars are 'Anananasnaja', 'Cordifolia', 'Hood River', 'Meader', and USDA selections '74-8', '74-49', and '74–55.' These females all need a male pollinator. 'Issai' is a self-fertile variety, but experience has shown that a nearby male increases fruit production.

An even hardier species is *A. kolomikta* 'Arctic Beauty', with cultivars that endure extremes of −40°F. Named females include 'Aromatnaya', '#1 Krupno-

pladaya', 'Pautske' (said to be the most vigorous of the Arctic Beauties), and 'Pavlovskaya'. Most of these produce fruit that is ready for harvest by the middle of August and all need a male pollinator.

Fruit/Harvest: Fruits are cherry-sized, dull green with a tangy-sweet flavor and fuzzless, edible skin. They have a lime-green flesh, similar to *A. deliciosa*, but produce far fewer seeds. Well-grown, mature vines bear hundreds of fruit in August and September. They do not store as well as those of *A. deliciosa*; about two months in a refrigerator is average.

Culture: *A. arguta* kiwis have the same basic cultural requirements as *A. deliciosa*. There seems to be a difference of opinion among experts on how many chill hours are required to produce abundant fruit on *A. arguta* vines. Estimates range from as low as 150 hours to as high as 800. The best course of action appears to be one of experimentation. *A. kolomikta* 'Arctic Beauty' requires between 200–300 chill hours. It prospers on the north side of the house in hot-summer areas, according to Northwoods Retail Nursery.

Propagation: Same as for *A. deliciosa*.

Pruning: Use the same techniques for *A. arguta* as described for *A. deliciosa*. For *A. kolomikta*, Northwoods' experts recommend only light pruning the first three years, then a heavier pruning of fruiting stems to regenerate the vine. Other experts advise that canes should be cut back to new growth each winter, leaving about eight buds, or fruiting spurs, on each cane.

Akebia quinata, Five-Leaf Akebia (4)   Another Asian import, this is a vigorous vine that grows to 30′ and is an excellent ground cover. In warm southern climates where it remains largely evergreen it can become a rank invader, but can be controlled by hard pruning from which it recovers quickly. In colder regions, it is semi-evergreen and not so rampant. A twining climber with sinuous stems, it is not plagued either by pests or disease. Fragrant flowers appear in clusters as early as April. Male and female flowers are separate. Females are purplish-brown and about 1″ in

***Akebia quinata,* Five-Leaf Akebia**

diameter. Males are somewhat smaller and rose-purple. Foliage is handsome and decorative, alternate and palmately compound, consisting of five oval to elongate leaflets, each about 2″ long.

Fruit/Harvesting: Fruits are black-seeded berries, 3″–4″ long and 2″ wide. The flavor is almost cloyingly sweet, and is favored in the Orient where the plant originates. Fruiting outside its native region is inconsistent unless female flowers are hand-pollinated. The male pollen from the same plant is not effective, so a different cultivar must be grown to provide for efficient fertilization of female blooms. When male flow-

ers are mature, rub them lightly against the pistils of the females. Fruit ripens in fall.

Culture: A sunny location is preferred, but the vine will prosper in partial shade. A soil rich in humus that drains well is best. Heavy clays should be improved with compost, peat, and well-rotted manure. Keep the medium just barely moist. If grown in fertile soil, no additional nutrients are required the first season. After the first year, a topdressing of a balanced organic fertilizer may be worked into the topsoil in early spring.

Propagation: Seed, divisions, and layers. Seeds should be germinated in a moist mix of sand, vermiculite, and milled peat moss in a warm location. Overgrown vines may be divided in late fall or early spring. Cuttings of current season's wood may be taken in summer, rooted in a shady spot, and either held in a coldframe over the winter or grown indoors in good light for transplanting in the spring.

Pruning: Vines grown in mild-winter climates often require hard pruning to keep the plant within boundaries allocated for it, since it continues to grow through the winter. Even when taken back to ground level, the vine recovers nicely. In other locales, heading back in fall or early spring may be required for control.

Ampelopsis brevipedunculata, Porcelain Berry (4+) This vigorous and beautiful deciduous vine from Asia makes a good cover for arbors and trellises and its dense foliage is suitable for screening purposes. Flowers are light green, borne in clusters, but not prominent. Leaves are alternate, lobed, toothed, from 3″–5″ long, and an attractive bright green. The vine climbs quickly to 20′ on twisting tendrils. Its outstanding feature is its colorful, edible fruit. Caterpillars sometimes target it, but these can be picked off and destroyed, or the vine can be sprayed with insecticidal soap. During damp weather, leaf spot may become a problem. Remove and discard (but not in the compost pile) infected leaves and apply a preventive spray of Bordeaux mix.

Fruit/Harvesting: Clusters of decorative, pea-size

berries, about ¼″ in diameter, are abundantly produced in the fall. Colors include white, pink, light green or turquoise, light blue, purple, and black. Berry flavor is often described as insipid. Harvest when fruits turn black and have "give" when lightly pressed between thumb and forefinger.

Culture: A sunny location with fertile, porous, moist soil is ideal, but the vine will adapt to light shade or part-sun/part-shade, as well as a broad range of soil types. Tolerant of cold extremes as well as wind. Requires a rugged support.

Propagation: Seed, cuttings, and layers. Take softwood cuttings in July and hardwood cuttings in September. Seeds can be germinated in moist sand, vermiculite, and perlite.

Pruning: Thin, shape, and head back in early spring, before the start of new growth.

Fuchsia corymbiflora, Peruvian Berry Bush (10)
Although usually considered only a showy ornamental, this is one species of Fuchsia from South America that bears delicious, edible fruit. Botanically, it is classified as a semi-climbing shrub rather than a vine, but it will ascend a trellis or similar support with some anchoring and direction, eventually reaching 12′. As do most Fuchsias, *F. corymbiflora* produces highly decorative flowers in spring and early summer. Those of this species are scarlet, 2½″ long, borne in long clusters. Leaves are opposite, oblong-lanceolate, and 3″–5″ long.

Fruit/Harvesting: Fruits are purplish berries that have the flavor of figs. They ripen in the fall.

Culture: Partial shade and fertile, humus-rich, evenly moist soil produce the healthiest, most productive plants. Work in peat moss, unless the native soil is already moderately acidic. Needs abundant irrigation during the season and benefits from an early spring application of a balanced organic fertilizer. If grown beyond its zonal limitation, treat *F. corymbiflora* as a tender perennial and house it indoors or in a greenhouse until frost danger has passed the following spring.

Propagation: Cuttings. Take softwood cuttings of new growth in spring or fall and root in a mixture of moist vermiculite and milled peat moss.

Pruning: Prune back to shape and control growth after fruiting. Cut back branches two thirds on vines wintered indoors, before new growth breaks.

Monstera deliciosa (also known as *Philodendron pertusum*), Split-Leaf Philodendron, Breadfruit (10)
This vigorous, evergreen vine is commonly grown as a houseplant and greenhouse species throughout the world and is a practical outdoor vine only in those mild-winter regions where the climate is similar to that of its native subtropical habitat. In an appropriate environment, the vine will ramble and climb until stopped by the pruning knife. It produces the familiar pinnately cut and perforated, handsome green leaves in abundance, and these achieve immense size in the garden—as broad and long as 2′–3′. As it matures, it produces long, ropy aerial roots along its main stems that will anchor themselves in the ground to support the vine's massive bulk and to forage for nourishment. It requires a strong support.

Fruit/Harvesting: Older plants produce flowers that resemble those of Calla lilies with a creamy-white spathe up to 1′ tall, encased in a white bract. This is the so-called "breadfruit" that is consumed as a delicacy in Mexico and Central America, the vine's native range. The spathe, which requires several weeks to mature, emits a pleasant aroma when ripe. Its flavor is a combination of banana and pineapple. Immature fruits that are harvested prematurely irritate the mucous membranes if eaten, so care should be taken to harvest only fully ripened fruits.

Culture: Prefers filtered sun to partial shade and a fertile, humusy, evenly moist growing medium. Can take copious volumes of water, provided there is good drainage. Usually blooms and fruits only in subtropical and tropical climates with high humidity levels.

Propagation: Cuttings. Take stem cuttings anytime with one or two nodes, or eyes, and press these horizontally into a mixture of moist sand, vermiculite, and milled peat moss. Rooting is hastened if cuttings are placed in a terrarium and covered with a sheet of glass or with plastic wrap. Poke several holes in the wrap for ventilation. If you use a glass cover, keep the top of the terrarium slightly uncovered so excess moisture can be evacuated. Set the terrarium in bright light (no direct sunlight) and a warm location.

Pruning: Vines usually require heading back periodically to check their rampant growth. Pruning helps keep a vine bushier, since it has a tendency to go leggy, dropping its lower leaves in favor of new top

Monstera deliciosa, **Split-Leaf Philodendron (with fruit)**

growth. New juvenile plants may be started at the base of old vines to screen barren stems.

Passiflora edulis, Passion Fruit (10) Probably the best known of the two dozen or so varieties in cultivation, this Brazilian native is the source of Passion Fruit juice. "Passion" has nothing to do with romantic ardor, but refers, instead, to the religious symbolism associated with the vine's flower. Its crown of filaments is said to represent the crown of thorns pressed onto Jesus' brow. The five stamens signify the five wounds inflicted upon his body—one in his side and one each in his hands and feet—and the 10 petals and sepals denote the 10 faithful apostles, with Judas and Peter not represented.

Flowers of *P. edulis* are about 2″ wide, white with a whitish-green corona, lavender in the center, and white at the tips. Leaves are three-lobed, deeply cut, 2″–4″ long and nearly as wide. Caterpillars are fond of the foliage (but not so much as they are of non-fruit-bearing Passion Vine species), and nematodes often kill plants the first year in regions where they are prevalent in the soil. (See Chapter 9 for organic controls.)

Fruit/Harvesting: Fruits are plum-size, egg-shaped, 3″ long berries containing many seeds in a tasty flesh. They are first green to greenish-yellow and change to a deep purplish-red and develop a pleasant fragrance when they ripen in mid- to late fall.

Culture: In their ideal environment, these are planted in the garden in full sun. Although tolerant of a wide variety of soil compositions, their preference is a fertile, humusy medium that is kept evenly moist in the summer and almost dry through the winter. The latter condition is rarely attainable, since winter rains are a fact of life in subtropical regions. They benefit from an early spring feeding of a balanced organic fertilizer worked into the topsoil after the first year of growth. Some gardeners use only a topdressing of well-rotted manure with good success. As a tendril climber, Passion Fruit vines climb readily up wires strung between verticals and on sturdy trellises made of 1″ lath.

When grown in cold-winter areas, the most effective technique is to confine the vine to a large (15–20 gallon) container in which a trellis has been installed. Before the first frost, wheel the container into a cool interior location in good light (or a greenhouse) and treat the vine as a houseplant. During its interior sojourn let the foliage go almost to the point of wilt before irrigating, to encourage a period of rest or semi-dormancy.

Propagation: Seed and cuttings. Seminal propagation is a hit-and-miss proposition, and many gardeners report only marginal success. The most productive method appears to be barely covering seeds in a mix of vermiculite and milled peat moss with bottom heat and tenting with either plastic or glass, as described for rooting cuttings of *Monstera deliciosa*. Far easier and quicker is rooting softwood cuttings via the same procedure, in early spring.

Pruning: For fruit production, the vine must be headed back periodically to redirect growth to sustaining flowers and fruit, rather than producing more vine. But, whether Passion Fruit is grown for fruit harvest or merely as a decorative accent, selective pruning is required each spring after the second year to open up the vine and frustrate its tendency to grow into an unmanageable tangle of dead and living foliage. Branches may be taken out at the juncture of another branch, or at the crown.

Seven other varieties in commerce bear edible fruit. Two of the most popular, commonly available from growers, are Blue Crown Passionflower (*P. caerulea*) and Maypop (*P. incarnata*). Both are root-hardy semi-evergreen to evergreen vines that survive extremes to 15°F. If top growth is winterkilled, both will recover from underground roots. Blue Crown Passionflower's fragrant blooms may be white, pink, or blue, 3″–4″ wide. The fruit is ovate, yellowish-orange, to 1½″ long, and is used as a flavorer for beverages, ripening in the fall. Like other passionvines, it is a tendril climber that may reach 30′, but should be headed back in summer for better fruit crops.

Maypop, an American native, bears 2″ wide white

***Passiflora edulus*, Passionfruit**

blooms with a lavender band at their center and ovate, yellow fruit in fall that is reminiscent in flavor of apricots. It is not as tasty as that of *P. edulis*. Like Blue Crown Passionflower, its top growth normally dies to the ground during cold winters and new shoots appear in early summer. For more abundant fruit production, restrict Maypop to 6′–8′ by heading the vine back in late summer. Both vines have basically the same culture requirements as *P. edulis*.

The other five Passion Fruit vines that bear edible fruits are Curuba (*P. mollissima*), fruit oblong-ovoid, 2½″ long; Giant Granadilla (*P. quadrangularii* 'Variegata'), leaves blotched yellow, fruit oblong-ovoid, 8″–12″ long; Sweet Calabash (*P. multiformis*), fruit round, 1½″ in diameter; Sweet Granadilla (*P. ligularis*), fruit ovoid, 2½″–3″ long; and Yellow Granadilla (*P. laurifolia*), fruit ovoid, 2″–3½″ long.

Rhoicissus capensis (also known as *Cissus capensis*), Cape Grape, Evergreen Grape (10) Distantly related to grapes (*Vitis* sp.), this South African tendril climber is an attractive accent for fences, for shading porches or verandas, and on lattice screens—with a bonus of decorative, edible berries. It is seldom seen north of frost-free areas, but it can be grown just about anywhere, with winter protection. Although it can reach 50′, 30′ is average. Mealybugs sometimes target it, but this pest can be controlled with strong jets of water or insecticidal soap. In spring, insignificant, small yellowish flowers are produced in clusters. Leaves emerge bronzy, then turn a bright, shiny green. They are round to kidney-shaped, with a rusty tinge on the underside, 4″–8″ long, on stalks.
Fruit/Harvesting: Glossy, reddish-black to blue-black, ¾″ diameter berries are borne in axillary clusters, in fall. They are commonly used in the making of jellies, preserves, and syrups.
Culture: Plant tubers in fertile, sandy, well-drained loam in a partially shady site. Like Clematis, Cape Grape roots must be protected from the heat of direct sun. Keep soil evenly moist and use a mulch layer 2″–3″ thick around the vine's crown. With adequate mulching and moisture, the plant will thrive in full sun. When grown in regions with harsh winter weather, grow the vine as a container plant. Install a trellis and control growth to maintain portability. Move plant indoors to a warm, medium-bright location or a greenhouse for the winter. Indoors it can tolerate considerable shade. Vines need to be guided initially to take the desired course.
Propagation: Tubers. Divide tubers formed on roots, in early spring.
Pruning: To control growth and keep the vine in bounds, head back in spring and fall. Pinching grow-

ing tips promotes bushiness.

Stauntonia hexaphylla, Staunton Vine (8) Native to Asia (Japan, in particular) this handsome and vigorous evergreen twining climber is a desirable cover for arbors, pergolas, and porches and is prized for its ability to create deep shade beneath its mantle of foliage and as an effective screen. Although it begins rather slowly, it gains momentum the second season and, if not headed back, eventually attains up to 40′ of height. It bears dainty, fragrant, bell-shaped, ¾″ wide flowers that are white with a mauve flush, in spring, around May. Foliage is alternate, palmately compound, with 3–7 ovate, untoothed leaflets up to 4″ long, radiating from the stems like the fingers of a hand. Largely pest- and disease-free.
Fruit/Harvesting: In fall, an abundance of 2″ long, ellipsoid, reddish-purple berries appear. These have a juicy, sweet flavor.
Culture: An ideal environment is one with long, hot summers with some shelter from the intense midsummer sun and strong winds. Its preference is for a moist, well-drained, humusy soil. It deteriorates in arid or mucky media. Cultivate into the topsoil well-rotted manure, in late fall. In early spring, feed lightly with a complete organic fertilizer.
Propagation: Seed and cuttings. Start seeds indoors in late winter in a mix of moist sand, vermiculite, and milled peat moss. Half-ripened wood taken in fall roots readily in the same seed-starting mix. Bottom heat and tenting hasten the rooting process.
Pruning: Some heading back is necessary when the vine is grown for fruit. Otherwise, prune to shape and groom and to eliminate tangled, intertwined growth and to remove deadwood, in early spring.

***Vitis* sp.,** Grapes (Various zones) Doubtless the world's oldest cultivated plant, the grape vine is still grown in virtually every country on earth. It has never been as revered in North America as it is in Europe—particularly France and Italy—where it is referred to simply as "the vine." One reason may be that it is not a vine one can plant and forget. It requires considerable nurturing and maintenance to produce a worthwhile crop, and Americans are not always imbued with the virtue of patience.

For its great bounty of fruit and its beautiful masses of handsome foliage, it is very much deserving of extra labor. Even without fruit, it ranks among the best of the ornamentals for the home landscape.

To enhance one's chance for success with grape vines, only cultivars that are regionally adapted to the growing zone should be planted.

Fruit/Harvesting: There are four types of grapes in cultivation:

American grapes (*Vitis lambrusca*), the so-called slip-skin grapes, which are largely pest- and disease-resistant and are hardy to about 0°F. Among these are 'Buffalo', 'Catawba', 'Concord', 'Delaware', 'Fredonia', 'Moore Early', 'Ontario', and 'Steuben'.

Muscadines (*Vitis rotundifolia*), which are well adapted to the hot, humid climate of the southern states of the U.S., sometimes referred to as the Cotton Belt. These are winter-hardy to about 5°F and prosper in the Middle and Upper South to about Washington, D.C. Good cultivars include 'Albemarle', 'Chief', 'Dearing', 'Hunt', 'Pride', and 'Southland'.

American bunch grapes are also well suited to Southern climates. Some of these cultivars are 'Blue Lake', 'Champagne', 'Ellen Scott', 'Lenior', and 'Lake Emerald'.

European grapes (*Vitis vinifera*), the Old World types. They are not so hardy as American grapes, surviving cold extremes down to around 10°F, and are often plagued by a number of diseases and insects.

French hybrids, which are crosses between European and American species. Trial and experience have demonstrated that these hybrids are more vigorous than native American varieties. In general, they need a growing season that is warmer and of longer duration than American cultivars, but they have an inbred

***Vitis* 'Thompson Seedless'**

resistance to cold (to about 5°F) that makes them adaptable to conditions in a broad geographic range. Some good performers among these are 'Baco Noir', 'DeChaunac', and 'Maréchal Foch' (reds); 'Aurore', 'Seyval', and 'Verdelet' (whites).

In the western U.S., depending on climate, cultivars of both *V. lambrusca* and *V. vinifera* are grown—cool-preference American cultivars in cool inland regions of the Pacific Northwest and some coastal areas, and heat-preference European cultivars and hybrids in the hot interior valleys of California and torrid regions of Arizona.

Depending on the type, grapes ripen at various times through the summer and are designated "very early," "early," "early midseason," "midseason," "late midseason," and "late," indicating their approximate harvest time. The best barometer, however, is the taste test.

Culture: Depending on the type of grape, there are specific cultural needs. In general, most will grow in a variety of soils, except for mucky, heavy clay. Deep (to 4'), fertile, sandy soils that drain well are ideal for all types. The site chosen should be open, with no nearby trees or structures that cast shade on the vines.

They need full sun to produce and ripen fruit, and a growing season of from 150–180 frost-free days.

Fertilization is largely unneccessary in the culture of grapes. If excessive nutrients are provided, the result, often, is too much vegetative growth. Occasionally, a nitrogen booster may be called for, but only if growth is weak or leaves begin to yellow off early in the season, when vines should be most vigorous.

Irrigation is important during a vine's first year, when young vines are getting established. An inch of water a week is usually sufficient. Mature vines are deep-rooted and somewhat drought tolerant.

Good air circulation around vines is important. Spacing between plants should be about 8'. In the

Vitis **trained by the cordon method**

VINES WITH EDIBLE FRUIT

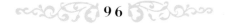

southeastern U.S., where heat and humidity create the ideal conditions for the growth and spread of fungal spores, muscadines are usually planted to a minimum of 15′ apart.

Grapes—especially European types—are susceptible to a number of fungal diseases and insect pests. Among the most common of these are the following:

Black Rot. Symptoms are shrivelled fruit, reddish-brown spots dotted with black specks on foliage. *Controls:* Remove and destroy infected fruit and foliage. To prevent future infections, spray vines with a Bordeaux mix before and after blooming.

Downy Mildew. Cotton-like growths on leaf undersides and yellowish splotches on upper surfaces. *Controls:* Same as for black rot.

Powdery Mildew. Foliage dusted with powdery growth on upper surfaces. Fruit may also be infected. *Controls:* Spray vines with sulfur or lime-sulfur fungicide to halt spread of disease.

Grape Berry Moth. Caterpillars and larvae of this pest feed on fruit. Larvae cut sections of leaves, roll them, and bind the flaps together with webbing into a kind of cocoon in which to pupate. *Controls:* If infestations are severe, spray BTK (see Chapter 9) to kill caterpillars. Pick and destroy leaves containing pupating larvae.

Grape Leaf Hoppers. Green or brown insects, ½″ long, that devitalize vines by extracting sap. Leaves appear stippled, then turn yellow. *Controls:* Spray leaves, especially undersides, with insecticidal soap.

Grape Phylloxeras. These pests are aphids that attack foliage and roots. Feeding on vine roots causes the formation of galls, which block the absorption of nutrients from the soil. This almost always stunts, then kills, the host vine. Leaf-feeding activity results in leaf galls the size of peas. These are not life-threatening but indicate the possible presence of phylloxeras in the root zone. *Controls:* No known effective solution.

***Vitis vinifera* 'Muscat', Italian Muscat**

Plant phylloxera-resistant cultivars.

Propagation: Cuttings and layers. To propagate cultivars of American and European grapes and those of French hybrids, take 12″ hardwood cuttings containing three buds, in winter. Set these aside to callus in moist sawdust. After frost danger has passed and the soil warms, plant cuttings in the garden so the top bud is at ground level.

Muscadines are increased by layering or softwood cuttings taken during the growing season.

Pruning: Grape vine pruning techniques appear to be

more difficult to master than they really are. Keep in mind that fruit is produced on current season's shoots that grew from canes of last season's wood. But the grape vines are not allowed to set fruit until the third or fourth year. By not permitting fruit to develop, the energy saved is reinvested into vegetative growth. Over this period, the vine is pruned back to train it into a strong, vigorous, productive plant for more bountiful future harvests.

The process begins when vines are first planted. Bare root plants, or rooted cuttings, are planted with a stake driven beside them for future anchoring of the vine. Soil is mounded up over the entire seedling. This encourages the development of deep rooting, which is crucial to the formation of strong vines that can tolerate periods of drought. Once shoots begin to appear, the mound of soil can be removed and replaced by 2"–3" of mulch.

Over the first summer, the vine is left to develop as much foliage as possible to sustain the roots. The first winter, prune the vine back to the thickest, most vigorous cane, taking out all others. Head this cane back to the three lowest buds.

When shoots that develop on the cane the following spring are about 8" long, choose one upright shoot to train as the vine's trunk and secure it in a loose loop to the support stake. Snip out the other shoots. Set another stake several feet beyond the first and string a sturdy wire between the two about 4' high. Over the following summer, when the shoot that is being trained as the trunk reaches a point about two inches below the wire, pinch back the tip. This will force the trunk to branch. When the trunk branches, select one shoot on each side to train in opposite directions on the wire and remove all other shoots that emerge. When the vine goes dormant in winter, prune the new growth that developed on the side shoots back to old wood.

Once vines have been trained for three seasons, different pruning methods are employed for different vine types. European types and muscadines are *spur* pruned, while American grapes are *cane* pruned.

Spur pruning involves cutting back side branches on lateral cordons to two buds. This is done in the late fall or early winter. The following spring the two buds will produce new shoots and each of these will bear fruit.

In cane pruning, four canes from the previous growing season are retained—two entire canes and two canes pruned back to two buds. The truncated canes are reserves that will replace the longer canes once these have borne fruit.

Detailed information on pruning and maintaining mature grape vines is available from local U.S. County Agricultural Cooperative Extension agencies and a number of books.

Arbors and trellises adorned with grape vines provide bountiful harvests as well as summer shade.

VINES WITH EDIBLE FRUIT

6

Vining Ground Covers & Trailing Shrub Covers

Vining ground and shrub covers offer the homeowner a number of benefits that conventional turf grass cannot. Among these are the fact that they don't require mowing and other lawn maintenance chores (and the attendant expenses); their ability to cover steep slopes and inhospitable terrain quickly; their usefulness as an attractive transition from trees and shrubs to a flatter plane; and their capacity for adding a unifying theme to the garden in distinctive leaf textures and colors that helps achieve a planned, finished look in the landscape.

They have other talents as well. Their ability to spread rapidly makes them ideal for controlling erosion by binding together unstable soil on hillsides and banks with their extensive root systems. Also, a number of species are shade-tolerant, so they can be used under tree canopies where turf grass often fails and in other sheltered sites.

In keeping with the vining (and climbing/trailing) theme of this book, only ground covers, shrubs, and shrublike plants that have a vining or creeping habit are included here. You can find hundreds of useful and handsome non-vining ground and shrub covers that are commonly planted to define garden perimeters and fill barren spaces in the landscape. These should be considered, along with vining types, when planning verdant spaces, but they will not be discussed in this book.

Vining ground cover in flats is often cheaper and easier to establish than gallon container plants.

VINING GROUND COVERS

Nearly all plants that vine will also creep over flat or hilly terrain and when they reach an obstruction, such as a tree, shrub, or fence, climb up and over it. One of the rambunctious vines is the infamous Kudzu (*Pueraria lobata*), imported from Asia a generation ago to help control erosion in Georgia. It performed the task well, but then continued to march across hills and dales, engulfing trees, telephone poles, barns, automobiles parked for more than a day, even entire houses.

Today, it is humorously referred to as "the vine that ate the South," and its incursions can still be seen in several southeastern regions, where it often expands at the rate of 50′ a season. Even more astonishing is the fact that gardeners are still planting it. It has an almost indestructible root system that goes down several feet, making it difficult to eradicate once it gains a foothold.

None of the following vines has this "Jack-in-the-Beanstalk" characteristic, but a few may need occasional heading back to control growth.

Akebia quinata, Five-Leaf Akebia (4) A bold ground cover or a graceful vine, Akebia is a problem-free plant native to the Orient and hardy to about −20°F. It gives a bonus of spring blooms, but it is its deep, emerald green, five-fingered foliage that recommends it.

Deciduous/Evergreen: Both, depending on region. Although deciduous in the north, leaves remain green into winter.

Flowers/Fruit: Clusters of separate-sex flowers, in spring. Males are purplish-brown; females, violet-brown. In its native Asia it produces edible purple fruit, 3″ long, in fall, but it rarely bears outside its habitat, unless hand-pollinated.

Foliage: Leaves are dark green, compound, composed of five leaflets to 2″ long on reddish-purple petioles.

Habit/Range: Twining climber that creeps over the ground, extending up to 15′ a season, and often mounds.

Culture: Prefers full sun, but is quite shade-tolerant. Grows well in light, slightly acidic soil that drains well. Can take some drought once established.

Uses: On erosive banks and slopes where the plant's deep-penetrating roots can stabilize soil, and in open areas away from other ornamentals, which can be engulfed by Akebia's rampant growth. Space seedling plants 18″ apart.

Propagation: Seed, cuttings, layers, and root division. Easiest method is by cuttings of either previous or current season's wood.

Pruning: Prune to control invasions into areas where it is not wanted, in early spring or early winter. Recovers nicely the following spring if cut back to the ground in winter.

Celastrus scandens, American Bittersweet (4) For a colorful winter accent and a fast-growing cover for banks and slopes, the native American Bittersweet is an excellent choice for northern and eastern gardens. It produces scores of orange-to-scarlet berries that persist all winter and contrast dramatically with the winter landscape. One must be certain to obtain bittersweets that bear both flower sexes or it will be necessary to plant two vines—one with male blossoms and one with female blooms—to get an abundance of fruit.

Deciduous/Evergreen: Deciduous, with persistent fruit.

Flowers/Fruit: Small, inconspicuous, scentless, white flowers, borne in clusters, in June. Fruits are yellowish, orange-to-reddish berrylike capsules, about ¼″ in diameter, produced primarily in terminal clusters, in fall. In late fall/early winter these burst open to display the bright red arils encasing the seeds. These cling through the winter, and birds have only a passing interest in them. Branches of fruited stems may be cut before the first frost, dried, and used effectively in floral arrangements.

Foliage: Leaves are an attractive lime-green, 2″–4″ long with toothed margins. They turn bright yellow before dropping in fall.

Habit/Range: A twining climber, American Bittersweet spreads efficiently as a sprawling vine to about 10′.

Culture: This vine's preference is a sunny to partially shady spot that has moist, slightly acid, well-drained loam. It usually fails in heavy soils that become boggy, but will prosper in clays and other media that drain efficiently. Once established, it tolerates occasional drought. It profits from a feeding of high-nitrogen fertilizer in early spring. Plants should be pruned back hard when first set in to encourage a vigorous start.

Uses: Takes well to rocky terrain and other problem areas. Provides an attractive cover for banks, slopes, and low walls.

Propagation: Cuttings and layers. Both hardwood and softwood cuttings are taken during the dormant season and rooted indoors in a mix of one part milled peat moss and four parts sand. Hardwood cuttings require bottom heat.

Pruning: In late winter, take out deadwood and stems that failed to fruit the previous season. Berries are borne on the current season's wood.

Two other Bittersweet species with similar culture

needs and geographic range are Korean Bittersweet (*C. flagellaris*) and Oriental Bittersweet (*C. orbiculatus*). The first is an effective barrier plant, armed as it is with punishing, spiny stems. It bears small, yellowish fruits and spreads 8′–10′. Oriental Bittersweet has rounded leaves 2″–4″ long that take on a bright yellow tinge in autumn and decorative orangish-yellow fruits in clusters that cling through the winter. It covers an area about 10′ in diameter.

Clematis **sp.,** (various appellations) (4/5) Five smaller-flowered species of this charming vine—among the most popular of the hardy flowering types—are suitable for use on banks and slopes and add a colorful accent to the landscape when in full flower. Provided they are planted properly and their roots are given the shade they need in summer, they are among the easiest of the vines to grow.
Deciduous/Evergreen: Deciduous.
Flowers/Fruit: October Clematis (*C. apiifolia*) (5) bears white blooms; Sweet Autumn Clematis (*C. dioscoreifolia robusta*, formerly listed as *C. paniculata*; 5), one of the most frequently planted of the small-flowered Clematises, has very fragrant white flowers that are borne in late summer to early fall; Virgin's Bower (*C. virginiana*; 4) produces panicles of small, white, 1″ wide flowers, usually in late summer. These precede plumy seed heads that are quite attractive in their own right; Traveler's Joy (*C. vitalba*; 4) bears greenish-white blooms, about 1″ wide, in panicles, from late summer to fall. It, also, has plumy seed heads that follow flowers; Italian Clematis (*C. viticella*; 4) has 1½″–2″ wide blue or purple blooms that are produced singly or in threes, throughout the summer. Varieties of Italian Clematis offer floral color options: 'Kermesina', red; 'Marmorata', mauve with darker veins, white specks; and 'Ville de Lyon', purplish-scarlet with a darker center.
Foliage: Leaves are opposite and generally pinnately compound, with 3–5 leaflets; some are lobed. Sweet Autumn's glossy, dark-green leaves are the most ornamentally effective of these species.

Habit/Range: Climbing, rambling with twining petioles, to 30′.
Culture: Clematises excel in full sun, but with their roots shaded—either by the application of mulches, or by the proximity of other plants whose foliage shades the soil around their crowns. Most prefer a moist, well-drained, light growing medium that is slightly alkaline to neutral on the pH scale (7.0). The addition of lime will amend overly acid soils. The planting site should be well cultivated for easy root penetration. Many times Clematises fail because they were shallow-planted. They should be planted with the soil ball containing the roots dropped 2″–3″ below grade, much like tomato seedlings.
Uses: Fine for rockeries, on slopes and banks, and used as a light garland draped over ornamental shrubs.
Propagation: Cuttings, layers, and grafts. Grafting requires skill usually beyond the ken of most gardeners. Softwood cuttings, taken in early summer, root readily in moist sand and vermiculite. Layers are often unsuccessful in cold-winter regions where the plant dies to the ground before layered sections root.
Pruning: May be headed back to about 2′ to rejuvenate, in fall.

Euonymus fortunei radicans (often sold as *E. radicans*), Common Wintercreeper (5) A handsome alternative to English Ivy (*Hedera helix*), this trailing ground cover is extensively planted throughout the U.S. and is hardy as far north as mid–New England. Even so, its cultivars, listed below, are more popular than the species. If given support, it will also climb. One pest plagues the plant and is difficult to control—Euonymus scale, which appears on stems as tiny bumps usually on the undersides or sides away from direct sunlight. The scales' feeding drains the plant of vigor, causing leaves to turn yellow and stems to die back. Control can sometimes be gained, if infestation is caught early, by scraping off scales and spraying foliage and stems thoroughly with superior oil (also called summer oil). A second application may be necessary. In winter, apply a dormant oil.

Deciduous/Evergreen: Evergreen.

Flowers/Fruit: Small, greenish-white flowers of no ornamental value, appear in late June. These are followed by greenish-white or pinkish, nearly round fruits that split open in fall to reveal orange seeds that persist into winter.

Foliage: Leaves are opposite and ovate, stalked, leathery, 1″–2″ long, and an attractive, glossy green.

Habit/Range: Trailing branches often root where they touch open soil. Spreads to several feet. Grows faster than smaller-leaved varieties.

Culture: Optimum growth results from a sunny exposure, but will thrive in partial shade. Not particular as to soil composition, although its preference seems to be a light, evenly moist medium that drains well. Usually does not prosper in hot, humid environments.

Uses: General-purpose ground cover substitute for English Ivy.

Propagation: Cuttings and divisions. Root softwood cuttings taken in July or hardwood cuttings taken in winter, indoors in a moist mix of sand, vermiculite, and milled peat moss. Plant may also be increased by division, in early spring, before growth begins.

Pruning: Weak-growing plants can be revitalized by shearing with a rotary mower whose blade has been set on high, in early spring. Prune to remove deadwood and to remove scale-infested branches.

The following varieties offer options in leaf color and size: Purple-Leaf Wintercreeper (*E. f.* 'Colorata') has 1″ long leaves that turn a striking dark purple in fall and winter; Variegated Wintercreeper (*E. f.* 'Gracilis'), a semi-trailing shrub, produces 1″ long leaves accented white, yellow, or pink; Kew Wintercreeper (*E. f.* 'Kewensis') is a slower grower with fine-textured foliage ½″ long; nice in rockeries between stepping stones; Baby Wintercreeper (*E. f.* 'Minima') is a dwarf with densely set leaves that are ½″–⅝″ long; Big-Leaf Wintercreeper (*E. f.* 'Vegeta') has leaves that are ovate to elliptic, leathery, to 1½″ long; new growth emerges chartreuse; large orange berries containing seed are produced in early fall and persist through the winter;

will mound and cover a 15′ square area by sending out side branches.

One additional species that is a useful and decorative ground cover is the deciduous Running Strawberry Shrub, or Running Euonymus (*E. obovatus*), a fast grower that sends out long, rooting runners covered with light green leaves, 1″–1½″ long, that turn a fiery red in fall. From August to frost, the plant bears decorative scarlet fruit. A native trailer, *E. obovatus* is hardy into central Canada.

Hedera helix, English Ivy (4)   Probably no vining plant is more used and useful in the landscape than English Ivy. Its neat, compact, evergreen foliage and fast growth make it a logical choice for covering large expanses of terrain, and it will even take the dense shade cast by trees. Three cultivars are hardier than the species and these are used in the extreme north: 'Baltica' has slightly smaller leaves accented with white veins and is usually planted in the colder regions of the U.S. and Canada; 'Bulgaria' (sometimes listed 'Bulgarica') closely resembles the species but is much hardier; and 'Romania' (also listed as 'Rumania'), which is similar to 'Bulgaria' in most respects. Three other cultivars are very hardy (to about −20°F) and are often seen in the Upper Midwest of the U.S.:

Hedera helix, **English Ivy**

***Hedera helix*, English Ivy**

'238th Street', 'Thorndale', and 'Wilson' (sometimes listed 'Wilsonii').

Deciduous/Evergreen: Evergreen.

Flowers/Fruit: Insignificant greenish flowers in clusters, in September. Occasionally, *H. helix* produces small, black berries.

Foliage: Most cultivars have leaves that are 3–5 lobed, alternate, and palmately veined, from 2″–3″ or longer. Tender cultivars offer greater variety, with variegation, marbling, fall color, and leaf shape.

Habit/Range: Clinger with aerial roots. Will ramble and root where stems touch open soil to 50′ or more.

Culture: Prospers in full sun or deep shade and a soil that is moist and humusy. Somewhat drought tolerant

once established, particularly the 'Bulgaria' cultivar.

Uses: Unsurpassed as a neat, tidy ground cover for sunny or shady situations.

Propagation: Cuttings and layers. Cuttings with two or three aerial roots attached may be taken during the growing season and rooted in a mix of moist sand and milled peat moss.

Pruning: Can be invasive. Will climb trees, shrubs, fences, and other structures; thus needs heading back periodically.

***Lonicera* sp.,** Henry Honeysuckle (*L. henryi*; 4); Hall's Japanese Honeysuckle (*L. japonica* 'Halliana'; 4) These two species are the best of the honeysuckles

Hedera helix **expands by rooting where its stems touch moist earth.**

for ground cover applications, but only in expanses of flat terrain where their invasiveness won't create control problems. Both are twining or prostrate in habit and remain mostly evergreen in warmer climates where they are sometimes considered a nuisance because of their aggressive behavior. Henry Honeysuckle is slightly hardier than Hall's and is often the favored choice in regions of marginal hardiness. Aphids occasionally infest them, and these can be controlled by light hosings or with insecticidal soap.

Deciduous/Evergreen: Deciduous to semi-evergreen in cold-weather areas; evergreen elsewhere.

Flowers/Fruit: Henry Honeysuckle's flowers are yellowish-red to purplish-red, trumpet-shaped, to ¾" long, often produced in terminal clusters, in late June. Hall's blooms are also trumpetlike, emerge white and age yellow and are lightly scented to very fragrant. They are 1"–2" long, usually borne in pairs in leaf

axils, from spring to fall in mild regions, June to September elsewhere. Both bear unremarkable black berries in fall.

Foliage: Henry Honeysuckle's leaves are opposite, ovate, from 1½"–3" long. Hall's are dense, opposite, oblong-ovate, 3"–4" long, and turn a bronzy yellow in fall.

Habit/Range: Twining climbers. Both can cover wide expanses and both will overrun ornamentals in their path. Hall's Honeysuckle will quickly root wherever stems touch moist soil. It also has a tendency to mound.

Culture: Quite adaptable, prospering in sun or shade and a wide variety of soil compositions. Once established, both can take some drought.

Lonicera japonica **'Halliana', Japanese Honeysuckle**

Uses: As ground and slope covers where their rampant growth is welcome.

Propagation: Division and cuttings. Take cuttings in early July and root in moist sand and vermiculite.

Pruning: Both cultivars may need heading back if they become invasive. In spring, thin by taking out deteriorated or hardwood branches. This will renew the vine and prolong its usefulness.

Two cultivars of *L. japonica* are considered by many gardeners to be superior to Hall's Honeysuckle and have about the same habit and zonal range. Purple Japanese (or Chinese) Honeysuckle (*L. j. chinensis* 'Purpurea') bears leaves and flowers ringed with purple. Yellownet Honeysuckle (*L. j.* 'Aureoreticulata') is so called because the yellow veining in its leaves resembles netting. It is not quite as cold tolerant as the other cultivars.

Parthenocissus **sp.,** Silvervein Creeper (*P. henryana;* 8); Engelmann Virginia Creeper (*P. q.* 'Engelmannii'; 4); St. Paul Virginia Creeper (*P. q.* 'Saint-Paulii'; 4). These popular disc-tipped tendril climbers are also decorative and useful ground covers, prized for their handsome foliage and moderate growth habit. The Engelmann and St. Paul varieties are extremely cold tolerant and are often planted without misadventure beyond their U.S. Zone 4 limitation. Sometimes plagued by mildew in warm, humid climates or during hot, rainy weather elsewhere. Sulfur dust is an effective control against the spread of this fungal disease.

Deciduous/Evergreen: Deciduous.
Flowers/Fruit: Inconspicuous flowers, followed by blue-black berries, ½" in diameter, carried in red-stalked clusters, in fall.
Foliage: Silvervein Creeper has five leathery, long, narrowly ovate leaflets, 1½"–3" long, that emerge bronzy scarlet and mature to a deep green, accented with white along the veins and with purple undersides. A bonus is intense red coloring in autumn. St. Paul Virginia Creeper produces alternate, palmately compound leaves with five elliptic-ovate leaflets up to 6" long. Engelmann Virginia Creeper's leaflets are much smaller than those of the species, while St. Paul's are set denser on branches. Both have brilliant fall color.
Habit/Range: Tendril climber/trailer with rootlike holdfasts. The Virginia Creeper cultivars will ramble up to 30', while Silvervein Creeper averages only about 20'.
Culture: Sun to partial shade. Leaf color is often more vivid in vines grown in light shade. Best growth is gained in moist, fertile, well-drained soils, but will thrive in a variety of soil compositions and moisture levels.
Uses: In addition to applications as climbers described elsewhere in the book, all make valuable additions to the landscape as ground cover accents in sun or shade.
Propagation: Cuttings are the most efficient method of increasing stock. Take cuttings in summer and root in moist sand, vermiculite, and milled peat moss.
Pruning: All three respond well to spring pruning to promote branching and bushiness.

TRAILING, PROCUMBENT SHRUB COVERS

There are a number of evergreen and deciduous shrubs that are appropriate for use as ground covers because they have most of the following characteristics:
• Ground-hugging, or prostrate, habit of growth
• Procumbent, or trailing, branches that extend for several feet, especially those that root where they touch open ground
• Stems that extend outward from the crown, particularly those that root as they go, to cover a wide circle
• Pendant, or trailing, branches and deep-growing, vigorous roots that bind together soil on banks and slopes, thereby stabilizing these declivities.

Unlike many vining ground covers which, at least in their juvenile stage, are herbaceous, shrub covers are woody, durable, and long-lived additions to the landscape. They offer a variety of leaf colors, textures, and sizes to complement or contrast with plants already in the landscape.

Like conventional shrubs, shrub covers may be used to unify the landscape and pull it together visually. For example, if the landscape is filled predominantly with conifers, needleleaf shrub covers can be added to harmonize with this theme. If the landscape is comprised largely of deciduous or evergreen broadleaf ma-

Companion ground covers of *Hedera helix* and *Lantana montevidensis* blend well together in warm-winter areas.

terial, use complementary shrub covers or, for textural contrast and interest, blend in some of the needleleaf species.

Whatever course is taken, the result should be a well-thought-out and harmonious design. Use shrub covers of the same species in combination, grouping three or four together, rather than choosing a variety of different species or stringing them out in a regimented row.

Finally, when shopping for shrub covers, stick to those that are acclimated to the climatic conditions where you live. Your nurseryman is a valuable resource in helping you select material that will prosper in your particular area. Bear in mind that zonal listings in this book and other references are only general guidelines. There are microclimates within zones whose temperatures may differ radically from the maximum-minimum extremes shown on zone maps.

Arctostaphylos uva-ursi, Bearberry, Kinnikinnick (2) Commonly seen from the bitterly cold stretches of central Canada to the arid, rocky terrain of northern Mexico, this useful, trailing evergreen is native to the northern U.S. and is valued for its hardiness and ability to stabilize sandy banks against erosion. It offers bonuses of handsome fall color and decorative winter berries. Two of the best cultivars are 'Point Reyes', which is more heat- and drought-tolerant than the species and is often planted on the West Coast, particularly in California, and 'Radiant'.

Deciduous/Evergreen: Evergreen.

Flowers/Fruit: Blooms are tiny (⅓″ long), bell-shaped, white with a hint of pink, in spring. These are followed by scarlet, berrylike fruits, ¼″ in diameter, that cover stems. They are borne in fall and persist well into winter, providing forage for birds.

Foliage: Leaves are 1″ long, entire, attenuate, ovate, and a bright glossy green. They are densely set on stems and take on a scarlet tinge with the first frost.

Habit/Range: Low-growing (8″–10″), wide-spreading (12′–15′) trailer whose prostrate branchlets hug the earth, where they often root. Effect is an attractive mat of dense greenery.

Culture: Prefers shade in areas where summers are hot and dry. The best plants are seen in cool, moist situations in sandy, slightly acid loam with excellent drainage, sheltered from the wind. Young plants require regular irrigation. Most are started from gallon-size containers. These transplants should be set in about 3′ apart, in spring in cold-winter areas; in fall in mild climates.

Uses: One of the best for sandy coastal slopes and other banks, where its culture requirements can be met. Also, can be used with good results as a cover for flat, rocky terrain.

Propagation: Sods of mature plants and cuttings. Large sections of matted plants are cut and taken up for transplanting into prepared areas of sandy, peaty soil. Hardwood cuttings, taken in late summer, may be rooted in a greenhouse or warm, bright indoor location.

Pruning: Seldom needed, except to rejuvenate old plants and to remove deadwood.

Cotoneaster dammeri, Bearberry Cotoneaster (5) Near the top of the list of this beautiful, vigorous species, Bearberry Cotoneaster is a low-growing (8″–10″ high), wide-spreading (to 10′) prostrate and cascading trailer that looks spectacular on slopes and banks or spilling over low walls. Two useful cultivars are 'Lowfast', which grows to 1' high and spreads nearly 2' each season, and 'Royal Beauty', which bears decorative scarlet berries. Both are hardy to −10°F.

Deciduous/Evergreen: Evergreen.

Flowers/Fruit: Tiny (½″ in diameter), white blooms appear in early June and, when clustered, make a nice accent. Fruits are showy, persistent, red berries, ¼″ in diameter, in fall. 'Coral Beauty' cultivar bears coral-colored fruits.

Foliage: Leaves are alternate, nearly oval, 1″ long, glossy.

Habit/Range: Prostrate trailer. Procumbent stems root at several points where they touch open ground. Spreads to 10' or more.

Culture: Prospers in full sun and moderately fertile, but not excessively acid, soil that drains well.

Uses: Ideal on banks, hills, and as a cascading plant to train over rocks, low walls.

Propagation: By division of crowded plants, and cuttings taken from July to September.

Pruning: None, except to remove deadwood. Snipped branch tips detract from the beauty of the plant.

Other valuable species are: Creeping Cotoneaster (*C. adpressus*), a slow-growing deciduous shrub that only reaches 1' or so, but spreads to 6'. It has dark green leaves, about ½″ long, that give good fall color. Fruits are intense red, about ¼″ in diameter. Hardy to −20°F (U.S. Zone 4). Creeping Cotoneaster is a fine, long-lived slope, bank, or ground cover whose branches root where they contact moist soil.

Rock Cotoneaster (*C. horizontalis*), one of the handsomest of the genus, a deciduous to semi-evergreen shrub that may reach 3' and cover about 15'. Its leaves are roundish, glossy bright green, ½″ long, and turn a decorative reddish-purple with the onset of cold weather. Flowers are pinkish, ¾″ in diameter, borne in June. Fruits are shiny red, about ¼″ in diameter, in fall. Hardy to −20°F. Use as an accent, barrier plant, or bank cover.

Cotoneaster **'Pendulus'**

Rockspray Cotoneaster (*C. microphyllus*) is a low-growing evergreen that may reach 3' with a 6' spread. Its primary branches trail and often root where they contact the ground if conditions are right, while its secondary branches are upright and arching. These are sometimes removed to maintain a low-growing appearance, but this is a matter of personal taste. Leaves are small (about ¼″ long) and lustrous dark green. Fruits, appearing close to fall, are rosy red and ¼″ in diameter. Hardy to −10°F. (U.S. Zone 5). Looks stunning on banks and hills.

SPECIAL NOTE: Cotoneasters are, unfortunately, often targeted by fire blight, a deadly bacterial disease, and three destructive insect pests—Cotoneaster webworms, lace bugs, and red spider mites. (See Chapter 9 for controls.) If any of these are prevalent in your region, it may be wise to consider another genus.

Gaylussacia brachycera, Box Huckleberry (5) Although it is one of the oldest of the New World plants, Box Huckleberry is not well known, despite the fact that it is a fine, durable ground cover. Part of the reason may be that it is a slow grower and most homeowners are looking for a cover that will grow with the speed of a weed. It is worth a look for those

Cotoneaster horizontalis, Rockspray Cotoneaster

who can wait a few seasons for the shrub to spread.
Deciduous/Evergreen: Evergreen.
Flowers/Fruit: Blooms are small, borne in loose racemes, and may be white, pink, or red. Fruits are bluish-black berries, in late summer.
Foliage: Leaves are alternate, elliptic to obovate, smooth and lustrous, to 2″ long.
Habit/Range: Creeping prostrate shrub that spreads (only 6″ a season) by underground stems that send up aerial branches.
Culture: Prospers in moist, peaty loam and partial shade. Declines in alkaline soil or heavy clays.
Uses: Gorgeous as a mat of green under conifers and shrubs.
Propagation: Division of creeping rootstocks, in spring, and by cuttings of softwood taken in July.
Pruning: None required.

Helianthemum mummularium, Rockrose, Sunrose (5) Except for the fact that it is sometimes difficult to transplant successfully because of its sensitive roots, Rockrose is a valuable, vigorous, maintenance-free trailing shrublet that gives two seasons of bloom. Related to *Cistus* sp., once established, it has the same tolerance for drought, which makes it an ideal choice for areas where summers are dry.

Deciduous/Evergreen: Evergreen to semi-evergreen, depending on climate.
Flowers/Fruit: Species flowers are yellow, about 1″ wide, five-petalled, and crinkly in texture, borne in June (earlier in mild-winter regions). Blooms last only one day, but are profuse. A wide range of other floral colors is found in the many cultivars in commerce: white, peach, apricot, pink, rose, and scarlet, as well as shades in between. 'Firedragon' bears reddish-orange flowers; 'Raspberry Ripple' has white and pink blooms; and those of 'Wisley Pink' are pale pink.
Foliage: Leaves are narrow, opposite, to 1″ long and either glossy dark green or dull, fuzzy grey.
Habit/Range: Mostly prostrate with trailing branches that often root where they touch moist soil, forming a thick mat of greenery. May mound to 1′. Each plant spreads to about 3′.

Helianthum sp., Rockrose

Culture: Full sun and soil that is neutral to slightly alkaline and well-drained. Peaty, acidic soil should be amended with lime. Needs moisture to get established, but then prefers drier conditions. In harsh-winter areas, protect evergreen foliage from dessication by covering plants with evergreen boughs or straw. Potted plants should be set in (3′ apart) without unduly disturbing roots. Cuttings from flats should be spaced about 18″ apart. Don't cultivate soil around plants once they are established.

Uses: Excellent for dry banks, slopes, and in rockeries.

Propagation: Divisions and cuttings. Good results come from rooting softwood cuttings of new growth, taken in July. Pot cuttings as soon as they are rooted to hold for future planting, to avoid root shock problems.

Pruning: To keep plants bushy and compact and to promote a second blooming late in the season, prune back hard after spring/summer flowering.

Juniperus chinensis sargentii, Sargent Juniper (4) Often rated the best of the prostrate ground cover junipers, Sargent Juniper is a durable, low-maintenance shrub with handsome blue-green foliage that contrasts well with other greens and broadleaf plants in the landscape. The cultivar *J. c. s.* 'Viridis' is

Prostrate juniper is a ground-hugging shrub cover that never needs mowing.

identical, except for its deep green foliage. In hot, dry summers, it is occasionally troubled by red spider mites. These can be discouraged by thorough and vigorous spritzings with the garden hose once or twice a week.

Deciduous/Evergreen: Evergreen.

Flowers/Fruit: Fruits are bluish berries, about ¼″ in diameter, in fall.

Foliage: Intense blue-green, scalelike, sharply pointed leaves.

Habit/Range: Nearly prostrate (to 18″ high) with expanding branches that extend to cover an area 6′–10′.

Culture: Full sun and light, well-drained soil. Becomes woody and loses some color in shady situations. Boggy conditions rot roots. Clayey soil should be amended with compost and gypsum. Tolerant of saline soils. When setting in plants, consider potential 10′ spread.

Uses: As an all-purpose ground cover in sunny exposures. Especially well-adapted to coastal slopes.

Propagation: Cuttings taken late summer through fall.

Pruning: None needed.

Lantana montevidensis (also sold as *L. sellowiana*), Trailing Lantana (9) In frost-free areas, this perennial evergreen prostrate shrub is unmatched in its ability to quickly cover a slope or large sections of the landscape where there is no foot traffic. It is prized for its profuse flowers that virtually cover the plant year-round, creating showy cascades and carpets of vivid color. It will freeze to the ground in regions beyond its zonal limitation, but will bounce back from roots in spring if deeply mulched after the first hard freeze.

Deciduous/Evergreen: Evergreen.

Flowers/Fruit: Species blooms are small (1″–1½″ across), lilac, in densely set heads borne terminally on long stalks. Seldom out of flower, ever in winter. Depending on the hybrid, other floral colors are white, yellow, orange, orange-red, pink, bicolors, and combinations. Fruits are inconspicuous black berries of no decorative value.

Foliage: Leaves are rough-textured, opposite, ovate, and dark green, about 1″ long.

Habit/Range: Trailing, vining shrub that mounds to 2′, with trailing stems that root as they go, to about 4′ long.

Culture: Sun, well-drained soil, and occasional, but deep, irrigation produce the most vigorous plants. Tolerant of drought, once established.

Uses: Stunning on slopes, banks, and tumbling over low walls. A superior, all-purpose ground cover in traffic-free areas.

Propagation: Softwood cuttings taken in spring root readily.

Pruning: In early spring, take out deadwood and prune back to prevent woodiness.

Rosa wichuraiana, Memorial Rose (5)   Memorial Rose is a perfect choice for erosive banks and unstable hills, and far superior to all other ramblers, many of which resulted from crosses between it and other species. Its habit is prostrate or trailing and, if not given support, it will send its procumbent canes close to the ground, where they anchor readily at various points. Mildew is an occasional problem. Remove afflicted portions and dust canes with sulfur to control

Lantana sp., Lantana

VINING GROUND COVERS & TRAILING SHRUB COVERS

the spread of the fungus spores. A good performing cultivar is 'May Queen'.

Deciduous/Evergreen: Deciduous in harsh-winter climates; evergreen in more temperate areas.

Flowers/Fruit: Bears white, five-petalled, slightly fragrant flowers, to 2″ in diameter, in clusters, July to fall. Fruits are red, about ½″ in diameter, in fall.

Foliage: Seven to nine round, glossy, serrated leaflets, to about 1″ long.

Habit/Range: Prostrate or trailing canes that root at several points where they contact moist soil. Each increases by several feet each season and, in combination, they cover several square feet.

Culture: Prospers in full sun or half sun/half shade. Most productive in deep, fertile, well-drained soil, but will adjust to less-than-ideal compositions. Intolerant of heavy, boggy soils.

Uses: Well suited to banks and steep, unstable slopes, but also performs well on flat terrain.

Propagation: Divisions, layers, and cuttings. Fastest results come from dividing mature shrubs. Cuttings, taken in midsummer, root readily in moist media.

Pruning: Prune to control and rejuvenate right after flowers fade. Selective pruning keeps shrubs compact and spurs production of vigorous, new canes.

Another variety that is widely used on banks to halt erosion is Glossy Virginia Rose (*Rosa virginiana*), a native American that is hardy to U.S. Zone 3. Its blooms are 1½″–2″ in diameter, magenta to pink, with five petals, in June. *R. v. alba* has white flowers. It spreads by underground stems and responds well to hard pruning when growth becomes too rank.

Rosmarinus officinalis 'Prostratus' Trailing, or Dwarf, Rosemary (7)   An attractive evergreen shrub, widely used in the western U.S. in both trailing and upright forms. It is hardy to 10°F, limiting its usefulness in northeastern landscapes, but it can be used here for borders and accents in containers plunged in the ground that are taken up and stored in a cool greenhouse or indoor location until spring.

Deciduous/Evergreen: Evergreen.

***Rosmarinus officinalis*, Rosemary, in bloom**

Flowers/Fruit: Tiny (½″) light blue blossoms in clusters that appear throughout the year but are most prolific in winter.

Foliage: Needlelike, grey-green, aromatic leaves closely set on stems.

Habit/Range: Nearly prostrate, with trailing branches that extend from 4′–8′. Older plants mound to 2′ or more.

Culture: Prospers in full sun and can survive searing heat. Not particular about soil composition, but medium must drain well. Does better in lean rather than overly fertile soil. Tolerates drought, once established, but needs periodic summer irrigation. Space gallon plants 2' apart; rooted cuttings, 1' apart.

Uses: Makes a nice border or edging plant, and quite attractive as a cascading shrub on banks and over low walls.

Propagation: Cuttings. Take 4″–6″ cuttings in fall, dip cut ends in rooting hormone, and set in rooting mix of equal parts sand, vermiculite, and potting soil. Keep rootings barely moist.

Pruning: To renew and control after winter flowering.

Vinca minor, Common, or Dwarf, Periwinkle (4)
A superb evergreen trailing shrub cover. *V. minor* is at the top of the list of "best" for fast coverage, versatility, and problem-free culture. It came to North America with European immigrants and has been used in gardens on this continent since the first lands were cleared for homes. Hardy and vigorous, it is content in full sun and light-to-medium shade.

Deciduous/Evergreen: Evergreen.

Flowers/Fruit: Species flowers are lilac blue, five-petalled, about 1″ in diameter, appearing in April. Cultivars offer floral color choices: *V. m.* 'Alba' bears white blooms; 'Atropurpurea', purple; 'Flore Pleno', purple, double; and 'Variegata' has dark blue flowers that are larger than those of the species and other varieties, as well as leaves splotched yellow.

Foliage: Leaves are opposite, 1″–1½″ long and an attractive forest green.

Habit/Range: Trailing, procumbent stems that radiate from plant's crown and anchor freely to form new plants. May reach 5″–6″ high, but covers an area several feet in diameter.

Culture: In hot, dry summer regions, does best in partial shade with regular, deep irrigation. In northern climates, thrives in full sun to part shade. During periods of drought, irrigate deeply and fertilize with a balanced organic plant food. Soil preference is a deep, fertile loam. Suffers in compacted and lean soils.

Uses: Works well with any landscape style, on flatland, banks, and under tree canopies.

Propagation: Divisions and cuttings. Take cuttings in early summer and root in a moist mix of vermiculite and peat moss.

Pruning: Head back in spring to rejuvenate weak plants.

Vinca minor

7

Climbing Roses

Climbing roses can soften the impact of towering walls and add a vertical blanket of color in the landscape.

Shrubs designated "climbing roses" are not technically climbers, in the same sense that twining vines are. They either produce tall, upright-growing canes or trailing, rambling branches that can be tied to supports for display. Left to their own devices, climbing roses and ramblers would develop into arching clumps with long, trailing branches.

Once started on a trellis or other open-weave support, branches can be woven through openings and need not be tied. Often those with thorns will hook these onto fence rails and other supports to hold themselves in place.

Climbing roses have been used for centuries to cover arbors, pillars, pergolas, fences, walls, and trellises. They are ideally suited to these applications, providing some of the most vivid floral color and captivating fragrances in nature. On arbors and pergolas they also create a shady and secluded retreat under their redolent and colorful branches.

Today, there are many improved natural climbing roses and sports from which to choose. In the pages that follow, 20 of the top-rated species are described, but dozens more could just as easily have been included.

When shopping for a climbing rose, apply the same criteria you would for selecting any flowering shrub. First of all, choose one that is acclimated to your climatic conditions. In hot, humid environments, resistance to mildew and other fungal diseases should be a primary consideration. Conversely, in areas of harsh winter weather with long periods of below-freezing temperatures, hardiness is of paramount importance.

Next, evaluate whether or not the climber you want to grow is right for the location you've selected. Factors that should be weighed are exposure (too shady or windswept), conflicts in color contrasts with existing material, and insufficient space to accommodate the plant's growth potential.

Finally, know the rose's blooming habit. When does it flower? For how long? Is there a strong repeat later in the season? Are the blooms fragrant?

In cold-winter regions, roses are offered for sale in early spring. In frost-free areas, where the shrubs can be planted in either season, they are available in fall and spring.

Roses are prepared for the marketplace either as containerized or bare root shrubs. Bare roots were field or greenhouse-grown for a period of time, then dug up and packaged with their roots packed in damp peat moss, sawdust, or other moisture-retentive material.

Bare roots have two advantages over containerized ones. First of all, they are usually less expensive, which can mean a significant savings for gardeners planning an extensive garden. Secondly, they adapt better to their new environment than container-grown shrubs, which can be a bit resentful of having their roots disturbed while they are actively growing.

What Roses Need

Climbing roses are just as finicky about soil composition and pH, exposure, moisture, and fertilizers as other types. It should be understood at the outset that roses are not plant-and-forget shrubs that fend for themselves. Generally, they require considerable fussing over and nurturing to prosper, but the joy they give with their floral beauty and heady perfume makes the extra care they need worth the effort.

SOIL AND SITE PREPARATION There are three basic types of soil: sandy, clayey, and loam. Sandy soil is somewhat gritty and does not bind together when compressed. On the plus side, sandy soil drains well so that water does not build up around roots, a situation that can lead to rot. From a negative standpoint, moisture often passes through it too rapidly, taking with it nutrients, so roots don't have a chance to absorb sufficient volumes of either. This results in dehydration, poor root development, and stunting.

Soil that is largely composed of clay particles—commonly seen in the southeastern U.S. and portions of the Far West and Southwest—absorbs large volumes of water and, once it is saturated, repels any additional moisture so that excess water collects on the surface and around roots, creating a boggy condition that leads to decay. Overly saturated soil also blocks the penetration of oxygen to the root zone, further compounding the problem.

If experience has shown that the native soil is slow-draining, it is advisable to take measures to protect roots from the deleterious effects of sitting in water.

This may include adding dry wells—several inches of pebbles in the bottom of the planting holes and beds—so excess moisture percolates down and out of harm's way, or by installing French drains. These are created by burying 4″–6″ diameter PVC pipe, perforated every few inches with ½″ wide holes, under shrubs. Sections of pipe are linked and directed to gravity feed drainage water to a lower level in the garden.

Loam is the third soil type and the ideal composition for growing most plants. It is a combination of sand, clay, and other materials and is usually rich in nutrients. It may be acidic (or sour) or alkaline (sweet) and, depending on the type of plants grown in it, may need amending to accommodate the preference of a particular species.

Roses thrive in fertile, well-draining loam that is a bit acidic on the pH scale. On this scale, 7 is neutral, or evenly balanced between acidity and alkalinity. Anything above 7 indicates a higher alkaline content; anything below means greater acid content. Most rosarians recommend a pH rating of 5.0–6.5. The pH rating of soil may be determined by a simple soil test. This can be done by a soil-testing lab, sometimes by U.S. County Agricultural Cooperative Extension Services, or by purchasing a kit and doing one's own analysis. Corrections in alkaline soil are made by digging in amendments with high acid content, such as ground or milled peat moss. Overly acid soil is generally corrected by mixing agricultural lime into native backfill soil. In both soil types, the addition of superphosphate and well-rotted (composted) manures is also beneficial.

Beds and planting holes should be cultivated to a depth of three feet. A rototiller is ideal for working beds, but the job can be done with a spade, if one is energetic.

PLANTING CONTAINERIZED, BARE ROOT ROSES Roses purchased in containers require half the planting time that bare roots do. Carefully remove the plant from its container, taking pains not to allow the soil to fall away from the root ball. The planting hole should be 4″–6″ deeper than the depth of the can and twice as wide. On the soil ball, measure from the base up to the bud union. In areas of hard winter freezes, the bud union should be about 2″ below the finished soil level when planting is complete. In mild-winter areas, the shrub is planted so the bud union is two inches above finished grade. Calculate how deeply the plant should be dropped into the hole so the bud union is at the correct depth for your area, then add or remove backfill soil from the planting hole to achieve this position.

Roses are planted like any shrub. Once the correct depth has been gauged and the support on which the rose will be trained has been installed (if needed), set the plant in the hole and begin returning backfill around it, firming it with a piece of scrap lumber, until the hole is half filled. Then irrigate to settle the soil, wait until the water drains away, and continue adding soil until the hole is filled. Build a ring of soil around the rose 2″ high to act as a water-collecting basin. Finally, irrigate thoroughly again.

Bare root roses require more steps. Remove the plant from its packaging the day before planting, and

A mound is prepared for planting bare root rose.

Roots are splayed over the mound in a natural growing pattern.

examine its roots. Prune off any dead or broken ones. Then fill a container that is large enough to accommodate the root mass with muddy water and soak the roots overnight. This will replace some of the moisture lost by the plant in transit and storage. The mud will coat the roots and help seal them against further moisture loss.

When you are ready to plant, build a cone-shaped mound of soil in the bottom of the hole. This should be broad enough to splay the roots over in a natural growing pattern without crowding or bending and high enough so that the bud union will be at the proper level when the hole is filled in. A piece of lath laid across the top of the hole will help determine this. Before arranging the roots over the hill of soil, nip off any that are too long to fit without cramping, and install any support that will be needed.

Spread the roots over the mound, add backfill until the hole is half full, then follow the steps described above.

Once the shrub is planted, prune the canes, taking out any that are thinner than your little finger and leaving three or four thick ones. Pull up moist soil around the canes until only the top thirds of the canes are visible. This serves as a protective mulch against the damaging effects of wind and weather extremes. Keep transplants evenly moist, but not boggy.

When new growth breaks and the weather has moderated, pull the protective soil away from the canes and mulch around them with a 2″ deep layer of weed-free compost or other organic material.

FERTILIZING ROSES

Common practice is not to feed newly planted shrubs (or trees) for the first 4–6 weeks. The primary reason is that the root system is getting established and the corrosive effects of fertilizer salts can "burn" tender, new feeder roots. You *can* add about half a cup of bone meal, deposited in 2″ deep holes around the shrub, after planting. Bone meal is a form of slow-acting phosphorus, and this element builds strong stems and vigorous roots.

As a general rule, established climbing roses are fertilized just once a year, and this is done in spring as leaf buds begin to swell. Roses, like other flowering shrubs, need a complete fertilizer, which is one that contains the three major nutritive elements—nitrogen, phosphorus, and potassium, or potash. An explanation of how each of these elements nurtures plants is given in Chapter 9. A good complete fertilizer for roses is one that contains, in addition to the major elements listed above, many of the minor elements, or micronutrients.

IRRIGATION

There is very little difference between the moisture requirements of roses and those of other flowering shrubs. As a rule of thumb, shrubs need at least an inch of water a week (newly planted seedlings should be kept evenly moist) when growing vigorously and blooming. This can be in the form of rainfall or delivered by an irrigation system. Rain gauges, which measure the amount of water reaching a given area in which they are placed, are inexpensive and commonly available.

Rosarians prefer a variety of methods of artificial irrigation. Some prefer drip systems that deliver a measured amount of water over a specific period of time through thin tubing to emitters, or heads. The advantages of drip over other methods are that foliage is not soaked, which is important in periods of hot, humid weather when fungal diseases are prevalent,

Drip irrigation helps avoid fungal diseases.

and only the soil around the root zone is saturated, which means that water is not wasted on unproductive surrounding soil. This also means climbers may be irrigated any time without risking fungal infections.

Other rose growers are dedicated to soaker hoses, sometimes called "leaky pipes," which are perforated in several places along their length. Moisture seeps out in a low volume and eventually saturates the nearby soil. These may be coiled around individual climbers or strung across beds.

Still others opt for in-ground sprinklers and hand-held garden hoses, preferring to do their irrigating early in the day so foliage has a chance to dry before nightfall. Their perception is that overhead watering cleans the foliage of dust and discourages colonization by aphids and spider mites. Also, since foliage can take in moisture and nutrients through leaf pores, or *stoma*, some believe that direct irrigation invigorates climbers, especially on hot, dry, windy days when moisture is transpired by the foliage at a higher rate.

Whatever irrigation method is chosen, climbers should be ringed with wells made of mounded soil as far out as the drip-line to retain water until it can be absorbed into the soil. Furthermore, if a 2″–3″ deep layer of an organic mulch is used, it will not only keep the soil beneath cool and moist, but will also discourage weeds and improve the structure of the soil when it decomposes.

MAJOR ROSE PESTS AND DISEASES

Six destructive pests (aphids, caterpillars, Japanese beetles, red spider mites, rose chafers, and thrips) and three diseases (black spot, mildew, rust) may afflict climbers on occasion.

Aphids, mites, and thrips devitalize climbers by sucking sap from stems and foliage—especially new growth—causing yellowing, deformation, and even death. Aphids are also disease vectors, transmitting viral diseases as they feed. Caterpillars, Japanese beetles, and thrips (and their larvae) destroy plants by eating buds, blooms, and foliage.

Spider mite damage on rose foliage

Black spot, mildew, and rust are all fungal diseases that usually appear during periods of moist, humid weather. Once present, they can be spread by transmitting spores from infected plants to healthy ones by working in the garden and by both rain and irrigation water splashing spores onto nearby plants.

Black spot is seen on foliage as black specks or circular spots the size of a matchhead, sometimes ringed with yellow tissue. It can also infect stems, causing dieback.

Powdery mildew is characterized by a powderlike

coating on leaves, stems, and buds, making them look as though they have been dusted with talc. Although not as devastating as black spot, it can weaken shrubs and cause deformed flowers.

Rust generally first affects foliage and is evidenced by white or yellow spots on the upper surfaces of leaves. Orange pustules often appear on the leaf undersides. The entire plant may become infected as spores are dispersed by irrigation or rainfall, with the eventual collapse of the shrub.

Pest infestations and diseases must be dealt with as

Japanese beetle infestation on roses

Black spot disease on a rose

Powdery mildew resulting from overly damp conditions

CLIMBING ROSES

soon as they are discovered. If either goes unchecked, the survival of the plant is questionable.

Controls for both pests and diseases are given in Chapter 9. These are general recommendations. It is always advisable to check with a certified nurseryman or county agricultural cooperative extension service agent for specifics. When given a choice, always opt for organic, environmentally safe solutions to pest and disease problems.

Deadheading roses strengthens the shrub and promotes a more productive repeat blooming.

PRUNING AND TRAINING Climbing roses are never given the drastic treatment with clippers that other types may require. With the exceptions of removing deadwood, weak, twiggy growth, and diseased canes, climbers are not pruned during their first two seasons while the canes and roots are building strength. Keep after canes, lashing them to their supports and directing their growth in the direction you've chosen.

Once climbers are established, they should be pruned in very early spring to shorten to 3"–4" branches that flowered in the previous season. On both climbers and ramblers, remove any suckers that appear. These are adventitious stems that grow from the rootstock. To ensure that these do not reappear, carefully pull soil away around the crown area and expose the point of origin on the roots. Then clip them off as close to the root as possible, taking care not to sever the root. Then replace the soil and pack it down.

DEADHEADING Roses expend energy producing seeds and hips. Unless these are specifically desired, dead and dying blooms should be snipped off to redirect this energy into the production of more flowers and into strengthening the shrub. This is done about half an inch above the first pair of five-leaflet leaves.

WINTERIZING AND WINTER PROTECTION Deadheading is generally abandoned in fall to help induce dormancy and prepare the shrub for winter. Spent blooms are left in place beginning about a month before the first predicted frost. Even in frost-free areas, deadheading is stopped to rest the shrubs and help them rebuild energy for the next season's growth.

Since nitrogen fertilizers spur new growth, these should be withheld from roses beginning about 6–8 weeks before the first frost. Slow-acting phosphorous-based foods, such as bone meal, may be used any time.

Climbers require considerable protection from the damaging effects of freezing weather in harsh-winter climates. Common practice is to remove the bindings holding canes to their support and carefully bending the canes down to a horizontal position on the ground. Some gardeners prepare a trench next to the shrub to receive the canes, but this is usually not necessary, except as an extra precaution in the coldest regions or when marginally hardy varieties are grown beyond their zonal limitation.

The reclining canes may be gently lashed together in a loose bundle. Then they are covered with a 6″–8″ layer of soil from another part of the garden. This may be covered with evergreen boughs, burlap, or leaves. A stake should be driven into the ground at the crown and at the tips of the canes to show where the shrub is buried. When snows have melted and the weather has warmed, carefully remove the winter mulch in several places to determine if new growth is evident. If so, and if the danger of frost has passed, disinter the canes, taking care not to damage tender new shoots. Leave the canes in place and keep the mulching material nearby for a while to be certain there will be no more frosts. Then restore the canes to their support.

In areas of less severe winter weather, climbers can be protected by wrapping the lower portion of the canes with burlap and by mounding soil (again, from another area) to a height of 12″–18″ over the crown and lower portion of the canes.

NATURAL CLIMBERS

***Rosa* 'Altissimo'**

(Red)

'Altissimo'   Climbing Floribunda
ARS Rating: 8.8   Introduced: 1966

Flowers/Foliage: Large (4″–5″ wide) deep blood-red shaded crimson, single blossoms in trusses. Anthers are brownish-yellow. Slight fragrance. Good repeat blooming in fall. Thick-set, deep green leaves.
Height/Form: 8′–10′. Medium, upright growth.
Notes: European import that has become an American favorite. Looks dazzling on trellises against west-facing walls. Susceptible to black spot disease. Winter hardy.

'Blaze'   Hybrid Climber
ARS Rating: 7.7   Introduced: 1932

Flowers/Foliage: Medium (2½″–3″ wide), cupped, brilliant crimson blooms, semi-double. A wealth of midseason flowers and an ample repeat. Leaves are thick, medium green and semi-glossy.
Height/Form: 7′–9′. Upright, vigorous.
Notes: A cross between 'Paul's Scarlet Climber' and 'Gruss an Teplitz'. Adapts to virtually all areas and prized for its profuse flowering and tolerance of heat. Winter hardy and disease resistant.

Rosa 'Don Juan'

'Don Juan'
Climbing Hybrid Tea
ARS Rating: 8.6   Introduced: 1958

Flowers/Foliage: Deep, velvety red, double blooms, either borne singly or clustered on long stems, with a very heady fragrance. Hybrid tea-type flowers are 4″–5″ wide. Bears abundantly all season. Leaves are dark green, leathery, and glossy.

Height/Form: 8′–10′. Medium upright, narrow growth.

Notes: Excellent, long-lived cut flowers. Not reliably winter hardy, so requires protection. Disease resistant. Well suited to pillars, trellises.

'Dortmund'
Kordesii Climber
ARS Rating: 8.6   Introduced: 1955

Flowers/Foliage: Blooms are single, 3″–3½″ across, and are intense red with a white eye and very light fragrance. Flowers open flat to display a central boss of yellow stamens. There may be 18 or more blooms in each truss. Good repeat. Leaves are light green, glossy.

Height/Form: 8′. Vigorous climber.

Notes: Performs well on pillars, light trellises. Tolerant of some light shade. Both disease resistant and winter hardy. Produces showy red hips in late fall. Resulted from a cross between a seedling and *Rosa kordesii.*

Rosa 'Dortmund'

'Paul's Scarlet Climber'

ARS Rating: 7.0

Rambler/Climber
Introduced: 1916

Flowers/Foliage: Semi-double, medium red, cupped blooms with a hint of fragrance, borne in clusters, each bloom 3″–3½″ wide, unfading. Flowering begins in spring and may extend into fall. Classified as a not-recurrent bloomer. Leaves are dark green and semi-glossy.
Height/Form: 12′–15′. Medium, vigorous growth.
Notes: Durable and hardy, with easily trained stems. Excellent on arch or pillar, or makes an effective seasonal screen. Good disease resistance. From a cross between 'Paul's Carmine Pillar' and 'Soleil d'Or'.

(Pink)

'Blossomtime'

ARS Rating: 7.6

Large-flowered Climber
Introduced: 1951

Flowers/Foliage: Blooms are classically high-centered, double, medium pink with a deeper reverse, with a strongly fragrant tea scent, 3½″–4″ broad, borne in clusters. Abundant midseason blooming with a modest repeat.
Height/Form: 6′–7′. Mostly upright, medium growth.
Notes: Often chosen for pillars, trellises, or low fences. Canes very thorny.

'Coral Dawn'

ARS Rating: 7.1

Large-flowered Climber
Introduced: 1952

Flowers/Foliage: Fragrant, coral-pink blossoms, 4½″–5″ across, in clusters. Prolific midseason bloom with good repeat. Leaves medium green, leathery.
Height/Form: 8′–12′. Upright and vigorous.
Notes: A climbing floribunda sport. Canes thorny. Ideal choice for pillar or trellis.

Rosa **'Dr. J. H. Nicolas'**

'Dr. J. H. Nicolas'

ARS Rating: 6.5

Large-flowered Climber
Introduced: 1940

Flowers/Foliage: Heavily scented, rose-pink blooms, 4½″–5″ wide, high-centered form, borne in clusters of three or four flowers along stems. Leaves dark green, leathery.
Height/Form: 8′–10′. Upright, vigorous, slender growth.

Notes: An excellent rose for a short trellis or pillar. Both winter hardy and disease resistant.

'Handel'

	Large-flowered Climber
ARS Rating: 8.6	Introduced: 1965

Flowers/Foliage: Slightly ruffled, creamy pale pink, edged with deep pink, double blooms, 3½"–4" wide, with slight fragrance. These are usually borne separately on thorny stems, but also appear in clusters of two or three, and are high-centered to cupped. Abundant midseason bloom with good recurrence. Leaves glossy, bronzy green.

Height/Form: 12'–15'. Medium tall, upright, vigorous growth.

Notes: Blooms appear summer after planting and cover stems. Winter hardy and disease resistant, although sometimes prone to mildew in humid environments. Good on fences, walls, trellises, and pillars. Originated from a cross between 'Columbine' and 'Heidelberg'.

(Orange Blends)

'America'

	Large-flowered Climber
ARS Rating: 8.0	Introduced: 1976

Flowers/Foliage: Stunning coral-salmon double blooms, 4"–5" wide, even-petalled, classically high-centered, borne in profusion in clusters on new wood. Heavy, but not oppressive, fragrance. Good midseason bloom, moderately recurrent. Leaves medium green, semi-glossy.

Height/Form: 9'–12'. Vigorous, bushy growth.

Notes: Adaptable to all areas with good response. Received AARS award in 1976, one of only four climbers to do so in the last 50 years. Disease resistant and reliably winter hardy. Performs well on arbors, pergolas, trellises, and pillars.

Rosa 'Joseph's Coat'

'Joseph's Coat'

	Large-flowered Climber
ARS Rating: 7.1	Introduced: 1964

Flowers/Foliage: This tall Floribunda bears what may well be called the most florid, showy blooms of all roses. They are deep golden yellow, suffused with orange and cardinal red, double, 3"–4" wide, with a slight fragrance, borne in trusses on thorny stems all summer. Leaves are greyish-green and glossy, providing an appropriate background for the carnival of colors presented by the blossoms.

Height/Form: 10′ or more. Upright, vigorous growth.
Notes: With its sturdy canes, 'Joseph's Coat' may be treated as a shrub rose requiring no support, but it dazzles when it is trained as a climber on pillars, arbors, and fences. Can quickly cover a chainlink fence. Not reliably winter hardy and susceptible to mildew. Resulted from a cross between 'Buccaneer' and 'Circus'.

(Yellow)

'Golden Showers'	Large-flowered Climber
ARS Rating: 7.2	Introduced: 1956

Flowers/Foliage: One of the most popular of the yellow-flowered climbers, largely because of its free-flowering habit. Blooms are canary yellow, fading to cream with age, semi-double, 4½″–5½″ across, generally appearing singly in abundance, but often in clusters carried by semi-rigid, long, moderately thorny canes. They open flat and have a light fragrance. Leaves are a handsome dark, glossy green.
Height/Form: 8′–10′. Medium, upright, vigorous growth.
Notes: An All-America Rose Selection and Portland Gold Medal winner for 1957. Disease resistant, although occasionally infected with black spot. Winter hardy in all but harshest climates. A Floribunda climber resulting from a cross between 'Charlotte Armstrong' and 'Captain Thomas'.

'High Noon'	Climbing Hybrid Tea
ARS Rating: 6.7	Introduced: 1946

Flowers/Foliage: Blooms are deep golden yellow, fading to a lighter hue, with a hint of red edging. They are double, 3″–4″ across, with a faint, spicy aroma, appearing singly on long stems in a loosely cupped form. A reliable all-season bloomer. Leaves are dark green and leathery.
Height/Form: 8′–10′. Upright, vigorous growth.
Notes: This winner of the AARS award for 1948 is a source of long-lasting cut flowers. Both disease resistant and winter hardy, it performs nicely on a trellis or pillar.

'Lady Banks' Rose'	Climbing Species Rose
ARS Rating: 8.6	Introduced: 'Alba Plena': 1807, 'Lutea': 1824

Flowers/Foliage: Blooms are small (1″), double, sweetly fragrant, borne in large clusters on long canes,

***Rosa* 'High Noon'**

spring to midsummer. 'Alba Plena' bears white flowers; 'Lutea' blooms are yellow. Evergreen leaves are composed of 3–7 leaflets, to 2½″ long, and medium green.

Height/Form: 20′, with an 8′–10′ spread. Vigorous growth with long, pendant canes.

Notes: Not winter hardy, but resistant to disease, aphids. Wonderful effect on arches, tall pillars, and cascading over walls and fences.

CLIMBING SPORTS

(Red)

'Climbing Chrysler Imperial'
ARS Rating: 7.8

Climbing Hybrid Tea
Introduced: 1957

Flowers/Foliage: Large (4½″–5″), dark red, classically shaped blooms with an intense spicy fragrance, on long canes. Profuse midseason bloom with a modest repeat. Leaves thick-set, glossy green.

Rosa banksiae, Lady Banks' Rose

Height/Form: 10′–12′. Upright, vigorous growth.
Notes: A strong grower that is suitable for sturdy arbors, fences, and trellises. Susceptible to mildew.

'Climbing Crimson Glory'
ARS Rating: 7.1

Climbing Hybrid Tea
Introduced: 1946

Flowers/Foliage: Deep, velvety crimson double blooms, 4″–5″ broad, with a strong damask fragrance. Blossoms hold well, but shrub is slow to repeat. Leaves are reddish-green and leathery.
Height/Form: 10′–15′. Vigorous, upright, bushy growth.
Notes: Tenacious climber, but responds well to training as a bush. Prospers in warm locations. Sometimes prone to mildew.

(Pink)

'Climbing Cecile Brunner'
ARS Rating: 7.8

Climbing Polyantha
Introduced: 1894

Flowers/Foliage: Small (1½″–2″) shell-pink, double blooms with a light tea scent, in clusters early in the season. Modest recurrence. Flowers have the classic hybrid tea form. Leaves are dark green and not abundant.
Height/Form: 20′ high with about an equal spread. Upright, very vigorous growth.
Notes: Does well on trellises and arbors, but also makes a nice accent as a cascader over walls and fences. Disease resistant and winter hardy.

'Climbing First Prize'
ARS Rating: 8.0

Climbing Hybrid Tea
Introduced: 1976

Flowers/Foliage: With blooms that are up to 6″ across, 'Climbing First Prize' produces one of the largest flowers of all climbers. They are double, deep pink, with a modest fragrance and high center, borne on long stems. Best show is in spring. Rather sparse

***Rosa* 'Climbing Cecile Brunner'**

through the summer. Dark green leathery foliage.
Height/Form: 8′–10′. Medium high, vigorous, spreading growth.
Notes: A fast, hardy, disease-resistant climber that looks marvelous on a trellis, fence, or arbor.

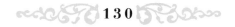

Rosa 'Climbing First Prize'

Rosa 'Climbing Iceberg'

(White)

'Climbing Iceberg'	Climbing Floribunda
ARS Rating: 8.8	Introduced: 1968

Flowers/Fruit: Blooms are double, with classic high centers, slightly fragrant, opening in a cupped form, in clusters. Good repeat. Leaves are semi-glossy and light green.
Height/Form: 15′. Vigorous, upright growth.
Notes: Susceptible to both black spot and mildew, but winter hardy. Charming on arbors, arches, and trellises.

***Rosa* 'Climbing Peace'**

(Yellow)

'Climbing Peace'
ARS Rating: 7.1

Climbing Hybrid Tea
Introduced: 1950

Flowers/Foliage: Lovely double, deep yellow blooms edged with pink, with a light fragrance, 4"–5½" across, on long stems. Classic high-centered form. Leaves are dark green, leathery, glossy.
Height/Form: 15'–20'. Tall, vigorous growth.
Notes: Disease resistant and winter hardy. Fast and strong, suitable for training as hedge, or for covering arbors and trellises. Long-lived cut flowers.

CLIMBING ROSES

Vines for Frost-Free Regions

A large number of vines, known only as somewhat temperamental houseplants or greenhouse and conservatory residents to gardeners in much of the United States and most of Canada, are routinely grown in landscapes in California, Florida, and coastal areas along the Gulf of Mexico.

While northern gardeners may sometimes perceive those who live in these benign climates as fortunate for being able to grow rare and exotic species in their gardens year-round, never having to cope with blizzards, ground freezes, and killing frosts, the envy is often mutual. There are scores of desirable ornamentals, berries, and fruit trees that can only be grown successfully in regions with long, cold winters.

Vines are popular plant choices in the southern states, California, and Hawaii for their ability to simulate a tropical paradise and provide shady relief from the oppressive heat of summer. Since many species of vines originated in the rain forests of Central and South America, most find the hot, humid climate of the South, particularly southern Florida and the Gulf Coast, much to their liking, responding with vigorous, rampant growth. Those climbers that evolved in the semi-arid, torrid expanses of South Africa, Australia, and New Zealand are right at home in many portions of southern California, stretching from Santa Barbara to the Mexican border.

Several of the following subtropical, tropical, and warmth-loving climbers may be grown in areas well beyond their sultry habitats. This is accomplished by two methods—container culture and winter protection.

A surprising number of vines, even a few that are normally deep-rooted, grow satisfactorily in containers of appropriate size—usually, ones of 20–30 gallon capacity, such as half whiskey barrels and tubs made of plastic, terra-cotta, and wood. Potted vines may either be plunged into the ground or grown as portable patio/terrace accents, both of which are usually cut back severely in the fall and wintered indoors (or in a greenhouse) until the last frost of spring has come and gone.

There are, however, some vines that decline when their roots are cramped, and this is noted after the species description. Other tender vines have resilient roots that will survive freezing winters if protected by thick mulches much as one provides for tender roses. Then, while the stems aboveground may be quickly felled by the first killing frost, the root system survives, insulated against the cold by its blanket of mulch.

By no means do all tender vines tolerate having their roots frozen. The best source of information on which ones will survive winters with proper protection in your area is a local certified nurseryman. Before an investment in tender climbers is made by gardeners above U.S. Zone 9 with the expectation of overwintering them outdoors, a consultation with a local horticultural expert is advisable.

Antigonon leptopus, Coral Vine, Confederate Vine (8) Among the most abundantly flowering climbers for hot, humid, or dry areas, the Coral Vine is a pest and disease-resistant vine, evergreen in mild-winter regions, semi-evergreen elsewhere. Its edible tuberous roots are a staple in the diet of some Mexican and Central American cultures, where it originates.

Flowers/Fruit: Trailing axillary sprays of up to 15 tiny (⅜″ long), pink blooms are borne profusely, summer to fall. There is also a white form. Blooms are long-lived cut flowers.

Foliage: Leaves are dark green, alternate, arrow- to heart-shaped, from 2″–5″ long, becoming very dense at vine's maturity.

Height/Habit: To 40′. Tendril-bearing climber.

Culture: Position Coral Vine in full sun in the hottest spot in the garden. It doesn't want fertilizer and isn't particular about soil composition. In fact, it thrives in lean, unimproved soil where other subtropicals would quickly deteriorate. It requires ample moisture with perfect drainage while it is actively growing and only sufficient moisture to keep it alive when it is resting. Tubers need two growing seasons to produce dense foliage and vigorous growth. New growth requires guidance and tying off until tendril-bearing flowers appear. Usually survives temperatures as low as 15°F. In marginal areas, where it is left in the ground, cut back to soil level in late fall and mulch heavily to protect against frosts and freeze/thaw cycles.

Uses: As a cover for arbors, pergolas, fences, and walls, and as a seasonal screen. Will completely engulf outbuildings after a few seasons in frost-free areas where growth continues through the winter months.

Propagation: Seed, division of tubers, cuttings. Divide tubers at planting time. Take cuttings below stem joint with one leaf attached, in September.

Pruning: May be pruned back severely for control after flowering, in fall.

Beaumontia grandiflora, Herald's Trumpet, Easter Lily Vine (10)   In botany, *grandiflora* means large-flowered, and this stunning, woody climber from Nepal has some of the largest of all vining plants and produces them by the hundreds. It is not a vine for constricted areas, for it needs a great deal of space to spread its arching stems. Largely free of pests and disease.

Flowers/Fruit: Long (5″), fragrant, white trumpet-like blooms are abundantly produced in terminal trusses from spring through summer. Petal edges may be tinged a faint pink and throats are veined green. Flowers are reminiscent of Easter lilies. Fruits are long, cylindrical pods of no decorative value.

Foliage: Bold, evergreen, semi-glossy, dark green, obovate leaves up to 1′ long. When pruned from stems, they seep a milky, tacky sap, much like some *Ficus* species.

Height/Habit: To 30′. Semi-twining with arching branches.

Culture: Prospers in sheltered, warm, humid environments and in fertile, humusy, moist, well-drained loam. Deteriorates quickly in cold or dry conditions. Needs even moisture in spring when vigorous growth begins. Does not thrive in containers. Roots are intolerant of confinement.

Uses: A bold trellis or specimen vine. Can be trained on columns and posts to good effect and looks stunning on wrought-ironwork.

Propagation: Softwood cuttings root readily in moist sand, vermiculite, and milled peat in a bright, warm location.

Pruning: Needs hard pruning after flowering to force the production of flowering lateral shoots; but retain some old wood, since vine blooms on previous season's growth.

Beaumontia grandiflora, **Herald's Trumpet; Easter Lily Vine**

Bignonia capreolata, Crossvine (7) A native of Maryland, the Crossvine is a strong-growing, evergreen vine with woody stems that compensates for its short blooming season with prominent reddish leaf color in fall and persisting through the winter. Its common name derives from the fact that cut ends of stems show a cellular pattern resembling a cross. This is an undemanding plant that prospers in a variety of conditions.

Flowers/Fruit: Bears 2″ long, funnelform, reddish-orange blooms in axillary clusters of up to five, in May and June. Fruits are narrow, flattened pods, to 7″ long, of no ornamental value.

Foliage: Compound leaves are opposite and composed of two ovate leaflets, to 6″ long. These change in fall from green to reddish-green. Branched terminal tendrils have adhesive discs.

Height/Habit: To 50′. Tendril climber with clinging discs.

Culture: Very adaptable to a broad range of conditions. Thrives in sun, heat, and coastal environments, as well as semi-arid atmospheres. Tolerates cold, but succumbs to extended freezes. Not bothered by wind.

Uses: Train on house and outbuilding walls, solid fences, perimeter walls.

Propagation: Cuttings and layers. Take softwood cuttings in early June from vigorous shoots and root in moist sand and vermiculite.

Pruning: Head back a few feet annually in early spring to promote vigorous new flowering shoots. Take out dead or weak-growing branches, also in spring.

Bougainvillea spectabilis, Bougainvillea, Paper Flower (9) This bold, showy, shrubby vine from South America is the most widely planted flowering climber in California and is equally popular from Mexico City to Rio. It is a mass of vivid color most of the year in frost-free climates, but especially in summer, when it truly hits its stride. Occasionally targeted by aphids, but these are easily discouraged with twice-weekly hosings. There are two forms of Bougainvillea, vining and shrubby. Shrub varieties don't climb but cascade with arching branches.

Flowers/Fruit: Flowers are hardly noticed tubes enclosed by three colorful bracts. Species colors are various shades of red, but varieties offer hues of white, salmon, tangerine, and a host of shades in between. One of the most floriferous of all vines, the effect is a solid sheet of color.

Foliage: Leaves are shiny or dull dark green, alternate, ovate to elliptic, to 3″ long.

Height/Habit: To 30′ or more. Twining climber with sturdy, thorned stems.

Bignonia capreolata, **Crossvine**

Bougainvillea **sp.**

Culture: Grow in full sun in all but torrid desert regions, where part-sun, part-shade is the ideal exposure. Irrigate regularly in spring and early summer, then cut back a bit in July to encourage prolific blooming. Although the vine is drought tolerant once established, it needs occasional drenching, especially in arid, desert climates. Best results are achieved when vine is grown in fertile, well-drained loam that is rich in humus. Wet, boggy soils spell disaster. Feed a balanced organic fertilizer in early spring and midsummer.

Prone to transplant shock from which some plants never recover. The best planting procedure is to re-move the bottom of plastic containers, set the vine in its prepared planting hole, make two cuts on opposing sides of the container and pull the two halves away from the root ball. If plants were grown in metal cans, drill holes in the sides and base and plant the vine, can and all. Eventually, the metal will rust away. Bougainvilleas thrive in large containers, so their zonal limitation may be pushed much farther north if vine is summered outdoors and wintered indoors before the first killing frost.

Uses: Absolutely unequalled as a canopy for arbors, ramadas, fences, walls, for shade and accent, and as a screen and barrier plant.

VINES FOR FROST-FREE REGIONS

Propagation: Cuttings and layers. Cuttings of half-ripe wood taken in late spring root readily in moist sand, vermiculite, and peat moss in a warm, sheltered location.

Pruning: Can be rampant. Often needs heading back to regenerate, shape, and direct growth. Take out canes at the crown. In marginal areas where it is struck by frost in spring, prune heavily and plant will recover.

Campsis × tagliabuana 'Madame Galen', Madame Galen Trumpet Creeper (5)   Often preferred over its parents, Madame Galen is a hybrid between *Campsis grandiflora* and *C. radicans,* and—although a fast grower—is not invasive or rampant. As with the species, its flowers attract hummingbirds. Aphids are fond of the vine but can be discouraged with periodic hosings.

Flowers/Fruit: Showy, salmon-red, tubular, 3″ long blooms with five spreading lobes at the end of the corolla, in loose racemes of up to 12 blooms, beginning in July (earlier in well-grown specimens). 'Crimson Trumpet' variety bears bright red blooms.

Foliage: Leaves are dark green, compound, and opposite, with up to 11 serrate, lanceolate leaflets, to 2½″ long.

Height/Habit: To 30′. Climber with aerial rootlets.

Culture: Best plants are grown in full sun (except in hot, arid environments, where it may need some afternoon shading) and moist, fertile, well-drained, humusy soil. Cold tolerant, but not so much as its parents.

Uses: Excellent as a cover for walls and solid-panel fences, but can be woven through lattice and tied to wire grids.

Propagation: Seed, cuttings, and layers. Seeds germinate without difficulty in a warm location. Take cuttings of previous season's growth in early spring and root in sand, vermiculite, and milled peat that is kept barely moist.

Pruning: Growing tips need regular pinching back to encourage bushy growth. To keep vine in bounds and

Campsis tagliabuana **'Madame Galen', Trumpet Creeper**

renew its vigor, head back and thin branches in early spring before appearance of new growth. Keep in mind that the vine blooms on current season's wood, so don't be tentative with the pruning shears if the vine is becoming weak or rank.

Clematis armandii, Evergreen Clematis (8)   This handsome vine, the only evergreen vining Clematis, has found great favor with gardeners in the southern portion of California and the frost-free areas of the Southeast, where evergreen plants are often more popular than deciduous types. Even without flowers, Ev-

ergreen Clematis makes a strong statement with its lustrous, dark green foliage. Occasionally infested with aphids, which may be controlled by frequent spritzings with the garden hose.

Flowers/Fruit: Fragrant white blooms, 1½″–2½″ across, borne in branched, leafless clusters, usually beginning by mid-May. Fruits are long, plump, plumed seed heads that develop in late summer and are somewhat decorative.

Foliage: Leaves are shiny, dark green, leathery, compound, with three ovate or oblong leaflets, 6″ long, 1″ wide.

***Clematis armandii,* Evergreen Clematis**

Height/Habit: To 20′. Climber with twisting petioles.

Culture: In hottest areas, part-sun/part-shade is the ideal exposure. Along the coast, position in full sun. As with other Clematis species, roots need mulching to maintain a cool, moist growing condition. Set transplants in deeply cultivated, well-drained soil amended with well-composted manure. Acidic soil requires liming to bring it close to a neutral (7.0) pH. Drop transplants 2″–3″ deeper than they grew in containers to protect stems and roots and obviate rot. Once planted, do not disturb roots by cultivating soil around their crown. Mulch well and sidedress in the fall with well-rotted manure and bone meal. May be grown successfully into U.S. Zone 7 with winter protection since it will not tolerate frosts and freezes. One option is to grow vine in a container and move it indoors or to a greenhouse until after the last spring frost.

Uses: Stunning when in bloom and grown on top of fences, arbors, pergolas, porch railings, and patio covers. Can be grown in containers.

Propagation: Cuttings and layers. Take softwood cuttings in late spring and root in moist vermiculite, milled peat, and sand.

Pruning: Prune after blooms fade. Vine blooms on old wood. Evergreen Clematis should be pinched at the growing tips to encourage denser foliage cover on lower portion of stems. Once flowers are spent, prune to remove tangled stems and to remove deadwood.

Clytostoma callistegioides (often incorrectly listed as *Bigononia violacea*) Violet Trumpet Vine (8)

Masses of lavender trumpet-shaped flowers cover this vigorous, rapidly growing evergreen import from South America for most of the spring and summer. It matures into a beautiful, strong, woody vine that, despite its height and bulk, becomes a graceful accent skirting the top of fences or clambering up and over a sturdy arbor. Not bothered by pests, diseases.

Flowers/Fruit: Bears 3″–5″ long and 3″ wide trumpet-shaped blooms in terminal pairs that are pale lavender with darker lavender in their throat, beginning as early as March. Vine is so floriferous, flowers

Clytostoma callistegioides, **Lavender Trumpet Creeper**

nearly obscure the foliage.

Foliage: Leaves are opposite and compound, with two glossy, oblong leaflets, to 4″ long. Leaves bear one terminal, unbranched tendril.

Height/Habit: To 50′ with 15′–20′ spread. Climber with leaf tendrils.

Culture: Prospers in both full sun and partial shade. Quite tolerant of heat and, with regular irrigation, semi-arid environments. Survives cold, but not prolonged freezing conditions. Roots will come through dips to 10°F if deeply mulched, making it possible to grow the vine into U.S. Zone 7. Prefers a slightly moist, well-drained, light, loam soil. Since its tendrils are not as strong as most others, and because of its massive bulk, vine will need tying off on its support to prevent it from collapsing upon itself. Feed a complete organic fertilizer in early spring.

Uses: May be trained vertically on trellises, wire grids, or posts, or horizontally on top of fences, along building eaves, and as a cover for rugged arbors, pergolas, or ramadas. Makes an effective screen. May be grown in large containers, but will need heading back to control growth.

Propagation: Cuttings and layers. Take cuttings from strong shoots in late spring and root in moist sand, vermiculite, and milled peat.

Pruning: Responds well to annual pruning in the fall to reduce bulk and ensure production of blooming wood.

Distictis baccinatoria, Blood-Red Trumpet Vine (9)   A vigorous, evergreen, long-blooming vine from Mexico, this is one of the most popular climbers in California and Gulf Coast gardens, prized for its vivid, blood-red trumpets. It is such a bold plant, it should be given a space of its own where the color of its blooms won't clash or compete with others nearby.

Flowers/Fruit: Scarlet, funnelform blooms with a yellow throat are borne on pendant terminal racemes. They average 4″ in length and appear almost continuously from the first warm days of spring to the first cool days of fall.

Foliage: Leaves are opposite and compound, composed of two leaflets, 2″–4″ long, often equipped with a terminal, branched tendril.

Height/Habit: To 18′. Twining climber with clinging tendrils.

Culture: Best vines are grown in full sun and in a moist, well-drained, fertile loam, but will thrive in part shade and a variety of soil compositions, so long as they are not boggy. Seedling vines should be irrigated often and fed a balanced organic fertilizer in spring, summer, and fall. Established plants need

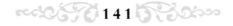

feeding only once a year, in early spring. Can be grown as a container plant. May be grown beyond U.S. Zone 9 with winter protection or when treated as an indoor-outdoor vine.

Uses: Absolutely smashing on high fences, walls, arbors, and trellises. A bold and decorative accent and specimen plant.

Propagation: Cuttings and layers. Take cutting of vigorous shoots in early June and root in moist sand, vermiculite, and milled peat.

Pruning: Common practice is to take the vine back annually after last flowers fade in fall, to maintain control and to revitalize. Tends to become top-heavy.

Ficus pumila, Creeping Fig (9)   An evergreen vine of great value for quickly covering cement block, slumpstone, and other walls in frost-free regions with a mantle of greenery. It is extensively used in California, where climatic conditions are ideal for it. Matures to a solid sheet of greenery, almost completely obscuring the surface on which it is grown.

Flowers/Fruit: Flowers are inconspicuous and of no ornamental value. Mature stems may produce yellowish, pear-shaped fruits that are not in the least decorative.

Foliage: Creeping Fig produces two foliage forms. Immature leaves are oval and from ¾″–1″ long, alternate

Distictis buccinatoria, **Blood-Red Trumpet Creeper**

and entire. Mature foliage is leathery, oblong, and 3″–4″ long. Both are dark green. The immature form is usually preferred, but both in combination on a flat surface are visually appealing.

Height/Habit: To 40′. Climber with rootlike hold-fasts.

Culture: Partial shade preserves the deep green color of the foliage, but vine tolerates full sun as well as heat and benign coastal environments. Fertile, well-drained soil produces the most vigorous plants, but once established, plant takes periodic drought in stride. Recovers from light frosts. Heavy frosts and freezes kill it to the ground.

Uses: Unmatched as a producer of thick mats of greenery on walls and other flat surfaces. Young foliage creates interesting design tracery. Often used to soften impact of block walls.

Propagation: Cuttings and layers. Take cuttings of small shoots in spring and root them in moist sand,

Ficus pumila, **Creeping Fig**

vermiculite, and milled peat moss.

Pruning: In early spring and late fall, prune to promote vigorous growth and to prevent the development of mature branches, which detract from wall-hugging design traced by juvenile growth. Regularly remove any branches extending out from the stems.

Gelsemium sempervirens, Carolina Yellow Jessamine (7)   An evergreen American native that is also found from Mexico to Guatemala, Carolina Yellow Jessamine is a well-mannered climber and profuse bloomer, and one of the first plants to bloom in the garden in spring. It is prized for its long bloom period and its adaptability to many uses. Seldom bothered by pests or disease.

Flowers/Fruit: Flowers are funnel-shaped, brilliant yellow, to 1½″ long, and are borne singly or in clusters of 1–6 blooms, usually in leaf axils, in spring. In southeastern U.S. gardens with their mild winters, summer heat, and humidity, blossoming may be through the winter into spring. Elsewhere the cycle begins in early spring and continues into fall. Fruits are oblong, short-beaked capsules of no ornamental value.

Foliage: Leaves are opposite, entire, lanceolate, 2″–4″ long, glossy bright green.

Height/Habit: To 35′, but 20′ is average. Climber with twining stems.

Culture: Prospers in sun or light, open shade. Prefers a fertile, slightly moist, well-drained loam, but tolerates a variety of soil compositions. Although a warmth-lover, it can survive brief dips to 15°F. In early spring, feed with a balanced organic fertilizer. Needs a sturdy support.

Uses: Produces a beautiful blanket of color on arbors, pergolas, patio covers, and ramadas. Does well on trellises, fences, posts, and as a screen and ground cover. Adapts to container culture, which extends its range beyond U.S. Zone 7.

Propagation: Seed and cuttings. In late spring, take 3″ long cuttings of new growth and root them in moist sand, vermiculite, and milled peat in a warm, shaded location.

Pruning: After the flowering cycle, head back side shoots to rejuvenate the vine and prevent the messy, tangled appearance it sometimes takes on. Remove weak branches and deadwood, in fall.

Hibbertia scandens, Guinea Gold Vine (10)

***Gelsemium sempervirens,* Carolina Yellow Jessamine**

A native of Australia, this fast-growing, shrubby evergreen vine is well adapted to the similar climate of southern California, where it is frequently seen serving as a screen or used as an accent on patios. It is a long-blooming vine with dense foliage and is easy of culture. Occasionally infested with thrips.

Flowers/Fruit: Blooms are clean, bright yellow, 2½″ wide, and resemble small single roses with their flattened petals and many stamens. Flowers are borne singly at the end of short branches, first in May and continuing well into October.

Foliage: Leaves are alternate, obovate to lanceolate, a waxy dark green, 3″ long and 1″ wide.

Height/Habit: To 30′, with a 15′ average. Climber with twining stems.

Culture: Prospers in partial sun, especially in west-facing locations, but also thrives in full sun. The best soil composition is a fertile, well-drained loam that is kept evenly moist. Responds well to an early spring feeding of a balanced organic fertilizer. When grown in marginal areas, recovers well from light frost damage.

Uses: On trellises, fences, arbors, and patio covers and excellent as a living screen. Can be grown in containers.

Propagation: Make cuttings from young shoots and root under bell glass without bottom heat in moist sand, milled peat, and vermiculite.

Pruning: Vine's habit is to become rangy and un-

***Hibbertia scandens,* Guinea Gold Vine**

kempt when allowed to run, so common practice is to keep it headed back to curb its rampant tendencies. Pruning may be done in very early spring, before bud set, or in fall, after floral production wanes.

Jasminum polyanthum, Chinese Jasmine, Pink Jasmine (8) One of the most fragrant of the more than 200 species of jasmines, Chinese Jasmine is a fast, vigorous evergreen climber with many uses in the garden. It is widely planted in California and the southeastern U.S. as an aromatic, trouble-free ornamental.

Flowers/Fruit: Fragrant flowers that are pink on the outside and white inside, about 1″ across, are borne in dense, axillary clusters from spring through summer. In mild-winter areas, blooming may span February through July.

Foliage: Leaves are compound, composed of 5–7 lanceolate leaflets, 2½″–3″ long.

Height/Habit: To 20′. Climber with twining stems.

Culture: Full sun and light, well-drained loam produce the most vigorous vines. Tolerates some afternoon shade. Not a particularly efficient climber. Branches often need tying off to support.

Uses: Quickly covers fences, trellises, arches, and arbors. Good accent close to the house, where floral fragrance may be enjoyed. An excellent container candidate.

Propagation: Cuttings and layers. Take cuttings of half-ripe wood in late spring, dip cut ends in a hormone rooting powder and use the aquarium technique described for rooting *Monstera deliciosa* cuttings in Chapter 5.

Pruning: Head back annually in late fall to control growth.

Another fine species that has the same culture requirements, but limited in range to U.S. Zone 9, is Angel Wing Jasmine, *J. nitidum.* It bears clusters of very fragrant flowers, to 1½″ long, that are white above and purplish underneath. Leaves are shiny, leathery, dark green, ovate, to 3″ long. Like *J. polyanthum,* its stems need securing to supports. It attains

Jasminum polyanthum, **Chinese Jasmine**

up to 20′ of height. Pinch out tips to keep vine bushy. Pruning is done in the fall after flowers fade to control and shape.

Lonicera hildebrandiana, Giant Burmese Honeysuckle (9) Its common name is apt, for this is truly a giant evergreen vine that can climb to dizzying heights of 80′ or more with its sinuous, ropy stems. Even its flowers and foliage are large when compared with most other vining plants. This is definitely not a vine for small-space gardens, but in large-scale spaces it can be used to good effect.

Flowers/Fruit: Flowers are lightly scented, tubular, light yellow aging to deep orange, each up to 7″ long, borne in pairs, summer into early fall. Fruits are green, round, and berrylike, 1″ in diameter, of no particular ornamental interest, forming after flowering cycle, in fall.

Foliage: Leaves are dark green and glossy, opposite, broadly ovate to elliptic, to 8″ long.

Height/Habit: To 80′, but 40′ is average. Climber with twining stems.

Culture: Partial sun in torrid areas and full sun in mild coastal locations. Although the vine prospers in fertile, evenly moist, well-drained loam, it will adapt to most soil compositions, except heavy clay. Tolerant of dry air, but suffers in strong winds. Survives temperatures to 25°F. Although top growth winterkills, roots will send up new spring shoots. Feed in spring and fall with a balanced organic fertilizer.

Uses: Ideal for draping across tall fences and cascading over high walls. Often trained up posts to second-storey balconies and under eaves.

Propagation: Cuttings taken in midsummer can be rooted in moist sand, vermiculite, and milled peat in a warm, shaded location.

Pruning: Head back or take out deadwood in late fall.

Another desirable honeysuckle species is the Goldflame Honeysuckle (*L. heckrotti*), a deciduous form that is hardy to U.S. Zone 5. It bears beautiful, fragrant blooms in terminal clusters that are scarlet-purple outside and yellow inside, from June to frost. Leaves are blue-green, oblong to ovate, to 2½″ long. Its twining branches ascend to about 12′.

***Lonicera hildebrandiana*, Giant Burmese Honeysuckle**

Lonicera heckrotti

Mandevilla **'Alice du Pont'** (also known as *M. splendens*, *M. amabilis*, *Dipladenia splendens*, and *Dipladenia amoena*), Mandevilla (10)   One of the most popular climbers in southern California and other U.S. Zone 10 regions, valued for its handsome foliage, vivid coral-pink blooms, quick, evergreen growth, and ease of culture.

Flowers/Fruit: Blooms are intense pink, trumpet-shaped and flared, to 4″ wide, profusely borne, spring to fall.

Foliage: Leaves are ovate, shiny, and ribbed, to 6″ long and half again as wide.

Height/Habit: To 20′. Climber with twining stems.

Culture: Full sun and fertile, humusy, evenly moist soil produce the best-looking specimens. Reduce irrigation from fall through winter. Top-dress in early spring with composted manure.

Uses: Stunning on trellises, posts, arbors, arches, patio covers, and ramadas. Thrives in containers.

Propagation: Cuttings of half-ripe wood taken in February root readily in moist sand, vermiculite, and milled peat with bottom heat.

Pruning: Rarely needs hard pruning, unless felled by frost. Pinch growing tips periodically to keep foliage dense.

A species better known beyond U.S. Zone 10 is

Mandevilla **'Alice du Pont'**

***Mandevilla laxa*, Chilean Jasmine**

Stephanotis floribunda, Madagascar Jasmine (9)
A woody evergreen climber native to Madagascar, this luxuriant and beautiful vine is the source of white, fragrant flowers commonly used in bridal bouquets and floral arrangements. Rarely seen outside the conservatory or living room in most regions, it is a desirable landscape climber in California and Florida. It is sometimes infested with mealybugs and scales, controls for which are contained in Chapter 9.
Flowers/Fruit: Clusters of white, waxen, funnelshaped, fragrant flowers with a 5-lobed corolla, borne in umbel-like, axillary clusters, from June through summer.
Foliage: Leaves are dark green, opposite, thick, leathery, to 4″ long.
Height/Habit: To 15′. Climber with twining stems.
Culture: Prospers in half-day sun with shaded roots and fertile, well-drained loam with average moisture. Survives short periods below 26°F, but preference is for warmth.
Uses: Very showy on short trellises, trained on openweave fences and lattice. Also thrives in containers and as both a greenhouse and indoor-outdoor specimen.
Propagation: Cuttings. Take hardwood cuttings with two eyes, or softwood cuttings with a heel (piece of older wood). Root in moist sand, vermiculite, and milled peat in a warm, shaded location.
Pruning: Seldom needed except to remove deadwood, in fall.

Chilean Jasmine (*M. laxa*), a fast, deciduous climber that also has twining stems. It grows to about 20′ and bears clusters of very aromatic white or pink-tinged, funnelform blooms that are up to 2″ wide, in summer. Leaves are opposite, entire, to 3″ long, carried on long stems. Has the same culture requirements as 'Alice du Pont'. Excellent on patio supports, open-weave trellises and arbors. Not a good container plant, since its roots are resentful of confinement. Range is to U.S. Zone 8 (root-hardy to 5°F).

Trachelospermum jasminoides, Star Jasmine, Confederate Jasmine (9) Although it is more a sprawling shrub than a vine, this lush evergreen species with its fragrant, star-shaped blossoms can be trained as a climber. It is one of the most frequently used plants in California and Arizona gardens and is also prized in the southeastern U.S., surviving heat, drought, occasional deluges, and hot, desiccating winds. Its secondary common name, Confederate Jasmine, comes not from the fact that it is ubiquitous in

the Southeast, but from its primary point of origin in Asia in what was once called the Confederate Malay States. It is slow to start, but grows moderately fast after its first season. Occasionally infested with aphids.

Flowers/Fruit: Sweetly scented, starlike or salverform white flowers with five corolla-lobes that are twisted and turned back, borne on long-stalked cymes. Blooms late spring through early summer (earlier in desert areas). Fruits are thin pods about 7″ long of no ornamental value.

Foliage: Leaves are oval to ovate-lanceolate, 2″–4″ long, shiny dark green.

Height/Habit: To 20′. Climber with weakly twining stems.

Culture: Partial shade in hottest areas. Prefers moist, well-drained soil of average fertility. Tolerant of most soil compositions, except heavy clays. Top-dress with well-rotted manure, in fall. If leaves begin to yellow, apply an organic nitrogen fertilizer, in spring.

Uses: Train on posts, open-weave trellises, and fences. Needs periodic tying off of stems to prevent vine from collapsing. Use a sturdy support structure. Prospers in containers.

Propagation: Cuttings and layers. Take half-ripe cuttings in early summer. Set aside to callus before dipping cut ends in hormone rooting powder and inserting into a mix of moist sand, milled peat, and vermiculite.

Pruning: When trained as a climber, prune to prevent bushiness, in fall.

Trachelospermum jasminoides, **Star Jasmine**

VINES FOR FROST-FREE REGIONS

9

Vine Planting & Maintenance

Vining plants (including vining ground covers and trailing shrub covers) are planted in the same seasons as shrubs and trees. In areas of winter freezes, the most auspicious planting time is spring, as soon as frost is out of the ground, after the temperature has moderated, and when there is no further danger of a killing frost. In frost-free regions, fall is often the favored time, with early spring running a close second.

Spring planting in bitterly cold winter regions assures the plant's roots will have a long season to become established before the rigors of cold weather set in. With evergreen material, it provides an opportunity for foliage and stems to toughen themselves against the stressing effects of frigid temperatures to come. Once the first seasonal freeze arrives, vines that are heavily mulched over will come through the harsh weather unscathed. When new growth is evident and the air has warmed, protective mulches are removed.

In frost-free areas, fall planting ensures that the vines will have several months of cool, moist weather to develop a strong, extensive root system before the arrival of summer heat. A vigorous root system is vital to the health and performance of a plant, and in cool weather a plant concentrates its energy into root production. Even so, there are many devotees of spring planting in the regions where winters are benign.

SITE SELECTION AND PREPARATION

As mentioned earlier, it is important to know the right exposure for a species to get the most it has to offer. This is especially true of flowering and fruiting vines, both of which usually need a sunny site to produce buds, blossoms, and fruit.

But a number of other vining plants that are said to need full sun do quite nicely in half-sun/half-shade, and a few reputed sun fanciers thrive in bright, open shade. It is always less troublesome to follow the recommendations of experts, but it is sometimes productive to do some experimenting of your own. For example, vines that are zoned for a warmer climate may frequently be grown in a colder one by planting them against a reflective and sheltering wall and giving them a winter blanket of mulch.

Also, within every zone are pockets of warmer air that permit plants listed for warmer areas to grow. These are called microclimates and they exist even in the most bitterly cold winter areas. A local nurseryman is a valuable font of knowledge on the subject of plant hardiness for your particular region.

Preparing the planting site correctly is crucial to the future health and response of a vine, as with any plant. Gardening lore instructs one, when planting vines, shrubs, and trees from containers, to dig a hole twice as deep and half again as wide as the container and mix the backfill soil with amendments such as compost and manures and—for acid-preference types—peat moss. Over the last decade researchers at several universities have determined that this advice needs updating. The current thinking is that since roots grow sideways as well as down, the planting hole should be two or three times as wide as the soil ball and only a few inches deeper.

Furthermore, tests have shown that improving the backfill with amendments is not only an unnecessary expense but may inhibit a plant's adjustment to its new environment. Studies show that roots introduced into enriched soil respond vigorously until they reach the unamended native soil. At this point, root development and plant growth are substantially reduced and the plant's vigor is never recovered to the extent it might have been if it had been started in native soil at the outset.

The exceptions are planting sites where the native soil is largely clay or sand. Clay soils trap too much water and block oxygen access. Overly sandy soils drain efficiently, but water passes through them so quickly, carrying away dissolved nutrients, that roots

Amendments for improving native soil

can deteriorate from dehydration and malnutrition. Vincent Lazaneo, a horticulturist with the University of California, Cooperative Extension, advises that, "If the soil is predominantly clay or sand, mix compost or peat moss into the backfill to improve it," pointing out that this is about the only solution to growing a healthy vine in a hostile site. When amendments are mixed with native soil, the proportions should be 30% amendments to 70% backfill.

PLANTING THE VINE

Container-grown vines should be carefully removed from their tubs by first irrigating them well, them compressing the sides of the container to loosen the root ball. Lay the tub on its side and tilt the bottom end up while tugging *lightly* on the trunk or stems. Jerking or pulling too vigorously can break the trunk at the crown.

Once the vine is out of its container, handle it as much as possible by the root ball.

The prepared planting hole should be just deep enough so that the soil level of the transplant will be about an inch higher than the surrounding grade. As the vine is irrigated over the next few months, it will settle slightly. One exception is Clematis, which should be planted with its crown 2″–3″ below grade.

Untangle any matted or girdled roots and drop the vine in its planting hole. This is the time to install any required support structure the vine will be trained on. Waiting until the vine is sprawling on the ground can be a frustrating experience for the gardener and a potentially damaging one for the vine.

Next, begin to add the backfill, tamping it snugly around the root ball with a piece of scrap lumber. New roots grow into soil only if it is pressing tightly against them. When the hole is filled halfway, irrigate to settle the soil. Wait for the water to drain, then continue adding soil without tampering it until the hole is filled. Irrigate again and build up a ring of soil around the dripline of the foliage, about 2″ high, to serve as a well to hold water until it can be absorbed. Then add a 1″–2″ layer of mulch.

Bare-root deciduous vines are planted in a slightly different manner. The hole is prepared the same way, but a mound of soil is built in the center to a height that will position the vine at the same level it was growing when it was uprooted and packed for shipment.

The night before planting, soak the roots in a pail of muddy water, which will help restore some of the moisture lost in storage and transit and get the vine off to a good start. Prune off any broken or decayed roots, then spread the remaining ones over the mound of soil in a natural growing pattern. Return the backfill to the hole, firming it over the roots with the heel of your hand until the hole is half full. Irrigate with about half a gallon of water and follow the procedures outlined for planting container-grown specimens.

Balled-and-burlapped vines are those that have been packed in a fertile soil mix and wrapped in burlap. These go into the planting hole the same way as container-grown plants, positioned so they are about an inch above grade. It isn't necessary to remove the burlap before planting; this would needlessly disturb

Overly clayey or sandy soil may be improved with amendments such as compost and peat.

Before planting bare root vines, soak the root ball overnight in water to restore lost moisture.

the roots. Merely release the ties holding the burlap to the trunk, fold it away from the crown, and tuck the edges under the soil. Within a few months, it will have rotted away.

Planting in Containers

A surprising number of vining plants may be grown in containers of appropriate size, as described in each vine's cultural notes. The advantages of maintaining plants in pots and tubs are many. This technique allows those without access to ground space to grow an impressive garden. Additionally, containerized vines may be positioned wherever desired, which is not always practical when they are grown conventionally. Finally, it makes it feasible to grow frost-tender species in harsh-winter climates without mishap. Subtropicals and tropicals may simply be trundled indoors or to a greenhouse location for the winter as soon as the first frost is forecast.

Ideal containers for vines are those of adequate size,

Prune off damaged or rotted roots.

Make sure the vine is planted at the proper depth.

usually from 10–30-gallon capacity with enough holes in the bottom to ensure efficient drainage, which is of paramount importance. They will also require a saucer of appropriate size to catch drainage water, which should not be allowed to stand in the basins for very long because of the danger of root rot.

Mix a custom planting blend following the recommendation for the vine in the cultural notes or ask a nurseryman for advice. For most vines, a light medium consisting of packaged potting mix, weed-free compost, one quart of horticultural grade (sharp)

sand to each gallon of medium, and two cups of vermiculite or perlite to every gallon of the mix is a suitable composition. For acid-preference types, pre-moistened milled peat moss should be added to the recipe in a ratio of 2-to-1 to the other ingredients. The inclusion of vermiculite or perlite is important, because soil in containers dries out more rapidly than soil in the garden. Both trap and hold water, which helps keep the mix adequately moist for a much longer period.

A traditional practice has been to put rocks or

As with bare root vines, create a mound of soil in the bottom of the planting hole.

Once roots are spread over the mound, refill the hole halfway, then water to settle soil around the root ball.

shards from broken clay pots in the bottom of containers to prevent roots from blocking drainage holes. This is not a good practice for vines grown outdoors. Using these materials creates nooks in the bases for root-chewing insects, such as crickets and beetles, to hide and breed. A better technique is to cut a piece of fibreglass screening to size and set it in the bottom over the drainage holes. Once soil and vine are pressing against it, it blocks access to destructive insects while allowing excess water to drain efficiently.

At the time vines are planted, trellises or posts on which they will be trained should be installed. This allows one to train the vine to grow properly in the early stages of its development and will prevent root damage later on.

Dehydration is the primary danger to container-grown vines, especially in hot, windy weather when moisture in the foliage is drawn out through transpiration. Also, the sun beating down on the surface of containers can quickly dry out the mix. During periods of torrid temperatures, it may be necessary to irrigate potted vines every few days to replace lost moisture. The goal should be to keep the soil evenly moist but never soggy, which can lead to rot and other fungal infections.

Fertilize container-grown plants with restraint. A buildup of fertilizer in a container can cause a vine to deteriorate since there is no way for it to be diluted and dispersed, as is the case in a conventional garden. At the end of the season, flush out excess fertilizer residue with several drenchings of lukewarm water, then allow the mix to dry out almost completely before irrigating again.

Irrigation

Keep newly planted vines (including those grown in containers) well watered the first season, while their root systems are beginning to expand. Nursery-grown stock is packed and potted in coarse soil (coarser and more water-retentive than native soil), usually with perlite or vermiculite added. This is because the limited root system of young vines is not sufficiently extensive to forage in surrounding soil for moisture and nutrients. These must be delivered directly to the roots until they have colonized the soil beyond that in which they were packed.

Transplants may require more frequent irrigation during the growing season, as described above. Typically, at irrigation time a 1-gallon vine will need 1 pint of water and a 5-gallon plant, two quarts. During cool weather, the frequency of irrigation may be reduced, especially if there has been adequate rainfall.

Established vines normally prosper with 1″–1½″ of water a week during the growing season. Many vines, particularly subtropical and tropical species, thrive in evenly moist media, soil that is moist to the touch 2″–3″ under the surface. Use a moisture meter to gauge this.

Some thought should be given to how the irrigation water is delivered. In hot, humid areas, overhead irrigation is probably not the best solution since it enhances the already ideal conditions for the growth and spread of fungal diseases. A drip-irrigation emitter head staked near the crown wets only the soil in the root zone. By not soaking foliage, it obviates the problem of fungal disorders while conserving water.

For vines grown in other areas, overhead irrigation is often beneficial, not only giving roots the moisture they need, but also clearing the foliage of dust and other pollutants. This method should be used early enough in the day so that moisture on foliage has an opportunity to evaporate before nightfall.

Drip irrigation systems seem to offer the most efficient method of delivering water to vines, including those grown in containers. The systems are relatively inexpensive, durable, and commonly available at most garden centers and by mail order.

Fertilizers for Vines

Fertilizer needs are listed after each plant's description in the encyclopedia sections. With few exceptions, vining plants grown in fertile soil need very little additional nutrition to prosper. Many respond well to only a topdressing of well-rotted (composted) manure in spring or fall.

Those that require seasonal feeding should be given a complete, or balanced, organic fertilizer. A complete fertilizer is one that contains the three primary nutrients—*nitrogen*, *phosphorus*, and *potash* (or potassium). These elements are sometimes referred to as N (nitrogen), P (phosphorus), K (potash). They are always listed in the same order on fertilizer containers. Occasionally, only their percentage content is prominent. For example, a 5 · 3 · 1 fertilizer contains 5% nitrogen, 3% phosphorus, 1% potash and 91% inert or inactive ingredients. The most nutritious fertilizers also contain several trace elements that contribute to plant health; among these are copper, iron, manganese, and zinc.

Less expensive and more prevalent in garden outlets are synthetic chemical fertilizers, which have been overused in the environment with disastrous consequences. Runoff of chemical fertilizers used in agriculture has poisoned hundreds of rivers in the U.S. and is largely responsible for the decline of coastal waterways by spurring the growth of algal bloom, which smothers aquatic life and chokes out beneficial and native vegetation.

In addition, chemical fertilizers add nothing to the soil in which they are used, but they do act as a fast-response tonic to plants growing there.

Organic foods, conversely, nourish both the plant *and* the soil, eventually adding to the fertility and humus content. Detractors point out that in addition

Bordeaux mix on *Vitis* species

Applying "Tanglefoot"

to usually costing more, organics are low in nitrogen, one of the most important nutrients for lush, green growth, and are slow to act. All true. Organics *are* low in nitrogen, but if a plant is suffering from a nitrogen deficiency, a single organic fertilizer that is largely nitrogen-based, such as blood meal (10•0•0), may be used to correct the problem.

Natural fertilizers do, indeed, act more slowly. The fastest response one may expect is about two weeks, while synthetics produce visible results in as few as two days. But the quick greening one gets from using chemical fertilizers is a temporary one. Organics will produce similar results over a longer span and these results will be long-lived. As organics break down in the soil, they create a continuous nutritional system that nourishes plants over many years, to the point where no fertilizers, organic or chemical, are needed in the future to grow vigorous plants.

Following are some of the popular organic fertilizers and their contribution to plant physiology:

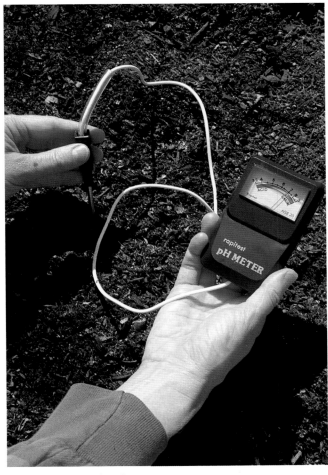

Testing soil pH level

Home soil testing kit

ORGANIC FERTILIZERS

High-Nitrogen	NPK Content	Benefit
Blood Meal	10·0·0	Promotes vegetative growth. Best in spring when growth begins.
Bat Guano	10·3·1	
Cottonseed Meal	6·2·1	
Fish Meal	10·6·0	
Phosphorus		
Bone Meal	1·11·0	Boosts flower, fruit production. Best when vine is flowering.
Rock Phosphate	0·3·0	
Potash		
Greens and	0·0·7	Stimulates vigorous root growth. Best in fall, when most root
Sul Po Mag	0·0·22	growth occurs.
Low-Nitrogen		
Barnyard Manures	1·1·1	Manures promote general overall nutrition. Seaweed stimulates root
Seaweed	1·0·5	growth.

Fertile garden loam

Timing of vine feeding is indicated in the culture notes after each plant's description in the encyclopedia sections. As a general rule, vines are fed in early spring to get them off to a good start. However, some are fertilized in the fall, especially in frost-free areas where new growth spurred by feeding won't be winterkilled. When in doubt about fertilizing schedules and volumes, consult a certified nurseryman or extension-service expert.

WINTER CARE

In harsh-winter regions, some vining plants need protection from the effects of bitterly cold, desiccating winds, as well as alternate freezing and thawing of the ground, which often causes heaving. In the latter instance, the entire root ball may be pushed to the surface, where it is vulnerable to freezes and drying.

Vines that are hardy in the north normally can sur-

Bark mulch as a winter protection against the freeze-thaw cycle

vive the frigid temperatures without special measures. Evergreen types may suffer some "burning," which is the result of cutting winds that draw the moisture out of the foliage. Where this is a problem, these vines should be confined to north-facing walls. In lieu of this, stems may be wrapped in burlap in winter and, where temperatures routinely drop to 0°F or lower, the stems may be packed with straw and then swathed in burlap.

In addition to wrapping vines to shield them from biting winds, it is possible to hill up soil over their crowns and cover this with compost—provided the root zone has first been irrigated and provided it is after the first hard freeze. Experience has shown that a well-watered plant is less likely to be injured by the cold than one whose roots are dry. The goal is to keep the ground frozen until spring, not to prevent the initial freeze. The danger to vines and other woody plants is from having their roots (and stems) periodically frozen and thawed by the mutable weather of winter and early spring.

As described earlier, for vines that are susceptible to injury from cold, such as those grown in areas where their hardiness is marginal or questionable, trench the plant while the ground is still workable. A trench is dug beside the vine deep enough to accommodate the stems when bundled together. The stems are released from their support and lashed together with stout cord. The roots on one side are either loosened or cut, while those on the other side are merely loosened so they are flexible. Then the vine is carefully laid down in the trench and covered with a shroud of burlap, a layer of soil, and, finally, a mound of compost. Stakes driven into the ground at either end of the mound will help locate the vine and obviate mishaps.

When spring arrives, and there is no danger of lingering frost or freezes, the vine is disinterred and restored to its support.

Tender vines and herbaceous types that can be grown in containers may be, as mentioned earlier, headed back and moved indoors or to a greenhouse before the first frost. Some may be grown as houseplants through the winter; others will go dormant. In both cases they should not be fed at all or given water beyond what is necessary to keep them alive.

Improving foundation soil

PESTS, DISEASES, AND CONTROLS

When compared with other garden ornamentals, vining plants are less vulnerable to attack by damaging insects and not so susceptible to diseases. This may be attributed to many factors, three of which are: (1) Many climbers have natural, inbred resistance to disease and insects. (2) Plant breeders have developed pest and disease-resistant cultivars that have largely replaced species plants that were weaker and more susceptible to attack. (3) There is a greater awareness of "problem prone" plants among nurserymen and knowledgeable gardeners.

Even so, insects and diseases can still threaten climbers, especially roses, and both should be dealt with as soon as they are discovered. Often, catching pest infestations before they colonize a plant and diseases in their initial stages can mean the difference between losing a plant and saving it. Once pests become entrenched and diseases spread, control is more difficult and injury to plants much greater.

Insect Damagers

Aphids Plant "lice" weaken then kill plants by sucking the life out of them. They are also vectors of plant diseases, injecting viruses as they feed. Aphids come in a variety of colors: white, yellow, green, brown, black, and pink. Woolly aphids resemble mealybugs. When food is plentiful, aphid "stem mothers" lay eggs. But when colonies become overpopulated and can no longer be sustained by the present food source, stem mothers give birth to winged young that then fly off to colonize a virgin plant.

Aphids have several natural predators. Chief among these are ladybird beetles, commonly called ladybugs, and convergent lady beetle larvae, aphid lions (green lacewings), hoverfly larvae, and predatory braconid wasps.

Aphid infestation

Controls: Initially, try hosing aphids off vines with a sharp spray of water. This won't kill them, but it will clean them from foliage and blooms. Once hosed off, they are not likely to return to the host plant. For heavy infestations, spray vines with insecticidal soap, or use pyrethrin or rotenone.

Cutworms There are several types of caterpillars called cutworms that chew through young, herbaceous stems, severing the top growth from its crown. Most are grey or brown and up to 2″ long. They overwinter

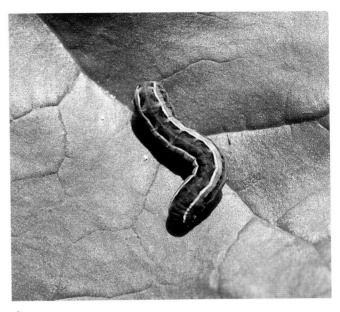

Cutworm

Convergent lady beetle larvae consume dozens of aphids daily.

in the soil and emerge in spring when the soil has warmed. After feeding, they burrow back under the surface.

Controls: Collars of cardboard or plastic pushed 2″–3″ into the soil around stems will block access to cutworms. Organic solutions include introducing parasitic nematodes or using BTK in the planting area a week to 10 days before transplants are set in.

Euonymus Scales   Prevalent in the northeastern U.S. and into southern Canada, this destructive pest

hitchhiked on some botanical import from the Orient in the last century. It is a serious threat to Winter-creepers and can also damage English Ivy and Bitter-sweets. It attaches itself to stems and the undersides of leaves and weakens a plant by extracting sap. Badly infested vines often succumb, regardless of how mature they are. Males are small, white, and narrow, about $\frac{1}{32}$″; females are brown and about twice as large ($\frac{1}{16}$″) and wider.

Controls: Scrape scales off with your fingernail or a dull knife blade and spray vine with a superior (summer) oil. In winter, use a dormant oil. Heavily infested vines may have to be taken back to the ground to eliminate the problem.

Grape Berry Moth   Larvae of this pest, which is prevalent in the eastern and northern U.S., bore through grapes and devour both pulp and seed and occasionally damage flowers. When they are ready to pupate they cut flaps of leaf tissue, roll them into a tube, and anchor the flaps with webbing once they are ensconced inside. They are nearly ½″ long and may be brown or green.

Controls: Keep area under vines clear of debris that can provide shelter for overwintering larvae. Snip off and destroy leaves containing pupating larvae. BTK will kill the caterpillars, but should be used only as a last resort.

Grape Leafhoppers Usually, these brown or green insects, which are about ½″ long, are not a serious threat to the health of grape vines. But, they can weaken vines by extracting sap, which causes stippling and yellowing. Infested leaves eventually turn brown.

Controls: Where numbers seen exceed a dozen, spray stems and both sides of leaves with insecticidal soap.

Grape Phylloxeras These aphid pests can threaten European grape vines by sapping their strength, resulting in stunting and poor fruit set. If phylloxeras attack roots, they cause galls that can ultimately kill the vine.

Controls: No known cure once damage has been done. Plant either American grapes or French hybrids, which are tolerant of this pest, or plant European grapes that have been grafted onto American rootstock.

Japanese Beetle Adult beetles have a glossy green body and coppery-orange wing covers. They colonize plants, often consuming everything from the topmost leaf to the lowest stem, leaving only the denuded skeleton. They also produce legions of white grubs with light brown heads that feed on roots, usually those of turfgrasses. Japanese beetles have an omnivorous appetite and damage a wide range of ornamentals and some food crops.

Controls: Respond to the first sign of beetle infestation. They can be picked off and drowned in soapy water or sprayed with rotenone. There is a Japanese

beetle pheromone trap available that does an excellent job of attracting and then trapping beetles. It is a plastic hanger with a bag underneath. On the hanger is placed a self-adhesive strip of pheromone, or sex attractant, bait. The beetles hit the scent bait and slide down into the bag where they are trapped.

Japanese beetles

Leafhoppers Although small in size (¹⁄₁₆″–½″) long), leafhoppers can wreak a great deal of havoc in the garden. Although there are over 2,000 species of leafhoppers, only a few are garden pests. The most common is the light green potato hopper with the characteristic wedge shape and wings carried high over the body. These sucking pests damage and often kill a number of ornamental and crop plants. They also inject toxic saliva into plants as they feed, transmitting viral diseases that usually are the death knell for weakened plants. When disturbed, some hoppers rapidly move sideways like a crab or leap into the air. Adults will usually fly out of harm's way. Hopper nymphs are pale, wingless, and hop acrobatically if approached.

Controls: Spray infested plants with insecticidal soaps, pyrethrin, rotenone, or sabadilla. Natural enemies include predatory flies and wasps.

Leafroller

Leafminers are larvae of several insects that feed by tunnelling between leaf layers of a number of ornamental plants. Their "mines" on leaves are sometimes serpentine, sometimes round, and are often the first indication that a leafminer problem exists. Look for clusters of tiny, round white eggs stuck to the undersides of leaves. Scrape these off and destroy them. Plants are severely weakened by the mining activity of these pests.

Controls: Snip off mined leaves and discard them in the rubbish bin. Spray plants with nicotine tea or neem, a natural insecticide extracted from the seeds of the Malaysian margosa tree (*Azadirachta indica*).

Mealybugs Common pests in southern and frost-free areas, but may also occasionally be a nuisance in northern gardens. Adults are about the size of a matchhead and have pink, segmented bodies coated with filaments of white, cottony fluff, which is a pro-

Mealybugs

VINE PLANTING & MAINTENANCE

tective wax secreted to form a shield against the drying effects of the sun. To some extent, it also protects them against pesticides. Their nymphs, which resemble adults, but are pale yellow, are as efficient as their mothers at extracting sap, which leads to weakened plants. They also excrete honeydew, which attracts ants that feed on the sugary substance. Mealybugs congregate in several generations on plants, usually in crotches and at leaf nodes.

Controls: Usually, these pests can be dislodged with a spray of water. Insecticidal soap quickly destroys them. Natural enemies include the mealybug destroyer, whose larvae also do an effective job controlling them, and the parasitic wasp, *Leptomastix dactylopii.*

Nematodes, Root

These minute, wormlike pests bore into roots and extract sap, draining vines of energy. While they are feeding, they inject saliva, which may transmit bacterial and fungal diseases. The vine's response to root injury is to form galls, much the same as we form scars to seal punctures in the skin. These galls interfere with the root system's ability to absorb water and nutrients efficiently. The results are weakening and, often, death of the vine.

Controls: Once nematodes have infested a plant's roots, there is no known response that will reverse the damage. The best course of action is one of prevention. Soil that is suspected of harboring nematodes may be treated with neem or it can be solarized by wetting it down and covering it with a layer of white or clear plastic through the summer to superheat it. Often this will kill nematodes in the treated area.

Rose Chafer

Although not a serious threat, unless infestation is extensive, these chewing insects should be controlled when seen, before they colonize a plant. Adults are brown beetles, about ⅓" long, with black undersides. Their larvae are tiny, white, and grublike. Adults chew flowers and lay their eggs around mid- to late May.

Controls: If several are seen on shrubs, spray with pyrethrin or rotenone.

Scales (Soft/Armored)

Scales damage plants both by feeding on sap and by injecting toxic saliva into their host. Most types also excrete honeydew, a sweet, tacky substance consisting mainly of undigested sap, that attracts ants that feed on it. If honeydew production is heavy, sooty mould fungus may develop, which further endangers the health of the vine. Hard-shelled (armored) scales protect them-

Scales

selves by secreting waxlike fibres with which they coat themselves, often combining coverings from previous molts. This substance hardens into a thick coating that is impervious to pesticides. Soft scales have a similar protective shell.

Controls: Because of their protective shells, scales are generally unaffected by sprays. Once they've formed their hardened skin, they become immobile, attaching themselves permanently to a feeding spot. The most successful method of dealing with them is to scrape them off with a fingernail or a metal nailfile, then spray the stem with pyrethrin or rotenone to kill any exposed eggs and nymphs.

Slugs/Snails Both of these destructive relatives of clams and mollusks can strip a young vine of foliage and sever stems from their crown overnight. They are serious garden pests in humid and temperate areas of the country yet are seldom seen in other regions. They come in a number of colors, but brown is the most common one. Slugs resemble plump, slimy worms with two pronglike antennae on their heads. Snails are nearly identical in appearance, with the exception that they carry a mottled shell on their backs into which they retreat when disturbed. Both are imperilled by the dehydrating effects of the sun, so they usually feed at night and on overcast days. They hide under foliage, containers, boards, and garden debris during the heat of the day.

Controls: Hand-picking and destroying is a quick solution. There are pellets and meals that are popular with some gardeners, but these pose a danger to the food chain and around children and pets. A good natural control is diatomaceous earth (DE), which is composed of the razor-sharp silica shells of algae called diatoms. It is rated harmless to humans and animals. Sprinkle rings of DE around the base of plants, if snail infestations are severe.

Spider Mites Not true spiders, but resembling them in appearance and by their web-spinning, these

Slug; brown snail

tiny pests thrive in arid conditions and damage plants by sucking sap from the undersides of leaves. The result is yellowing or stippling of foliage and weakened growth. They spin haphazard webs and these are usually the first indication of their presence.

Controls: Fortunately, spider mites are relatively easy to discourage. Spray plants thoroughly with a strong jet of water from the garden hose several times a week. If the problem persists, use insecticidal soap.

Thrips are not as great a problem as are aphids and caterpillar larvae, but they are equally destructive in large numbers. A fraction of an inch long, these yellowish-white to brownish-black insects and their nymphs rasp tears in foliage and drink the sap that oozes from the wounds, causing yellowing and weakening of the plant. Evidence of their feeding is silver streaking on foliage. Populations mushroom in late summer, so early control is imperative.

Controls: Before leaf-out and after the growing season, spray dormant oil on susceptible climbers. Yellow sticky traps, which are pieces of durable cardboard tinted yellow and coated with a tacky substance, attract and capture flying adults. When fruiting vines set fruit, spray vines with pyrethrin or insecticidal soap.

Whiteflies are almost microscopic insects that resemble tiny moths. They are prolific breeders that suck sap from the undersides of leaves of a broad range of ornamental and edible plants. When disturbed, colonies rise up in a cloud. One female can produce 300 eggs in a month. Both adults and nymphs feed on plants and often inject hosts with viral diseases.

Controls: One of the best weapons against whiteflies is the yellow sticky trap, which they find irresistible. Spray heavily infested vines with insecticidal soap, garlic oil, pyrethrin, or rotenone.

Diseases and Their Control

By far the most common of the three basic types of diseases infecting ornamental and crop plants (*fungal*, *bacterial*, and *viral*), fungal diseases are the ones that appear in vining plants with the greatest frequency. Usually, infections are spurred by environmental factors—moist foliage and cool, damp weather, wind-blown spores, and poor sanitation in the garden, in which decaying vegetation is allowed to collect around plants, creating a favorable breeding ground for diseases. Viruses are often introduced to plants by insect vectors, or carriers, which pass them on in toxic saliva as they feed.

There are simple steps to take to prevent fungal disease from getting a foothold in the garden. Never let one's plants "go to bed wet." If overhead irrigation is used in the garden, use it early enough in the day so moisture evaporates from leaf surfaces before sunset.

To avoid spreading diseases to healthy plants do not work around them when they are wet. Moisture is an excellent conductor of plant disease pathogens. If you prune or handle a diseased plant, wash your hands with soap and dip your pruning blades into a solution of 10% chlorine bleach and 90% water before working on other plants.

Finally, keep fallen leaves and fruit away from vines to eliminate breeding places for diseases and hiding spots for destructive insects. If pruned vegetation or fruit is infected, consign it to the rubbish bin, not the compost pile, where conditions are ideal for its spread.

FUNGAL DISEASES

Anthracnose First evidence of this disease are small, yellow spots of dead tissue that expand and turn brown or black. Decaying tissue drops out to leave irregular holes. Fruit develops dark, sunken lesions. Damp weather causes it to spread rapidly.

Susceptible plants: A number of woody and herbaceous plants.

Controls: Shop for anthracnose-resistant varieties. Clean up fallen debris. Once disease is evident, prune off affected foliage, sterilize pruning tools, then spray with a fungicide to halt the spread.

Black Rot This foliage disease begins as irregular light-yellowish spots that soon turn black. Other forms of rot may follow. Grapes shrivel into hard, raisinlike "mummies." Foliage becomes flecked with black and brown spots.

Susceptible plants: Grapes.

Controls: It may be possible to find rot-resistant varieties. Before disease develops on grapes, spray healthy vines with a preventive treatment of Bordeaux mix or other copper-based fungicide, before and after blooming. To halt the spread of the disease, dispose of infected plants.

Black Spot

A fungal disease prevalent in roses during moist, humid weather. It discolors leaves with black spots ringed with yellowing, necrotic tissue and also causes blistering on canes.

Susceptible plants: Roses.

Controls: Prune out and destroy infected leaves, stems, and canes. Once this disease gains a foothold, it resists control measures. Begin by keeping irrigation water off foliage. When infected plant parts have been removed, spray plants with sulfur or a solution of one teaspoon of baking soda in a quart of warm water. Repeat weekly.

Botrytis Blight

Cool, humid weather and poor air circulation provide the perfect conditions for this destructive fungal disease. Leaves of plants first show water-soaked areas that eventually turn brown as tissue dies.

Susceptible plants: Grapes, as well as ornamentals and herbaceous plants.

Controls: The best hope is to halt the spread of the infection. This is accomplished by improving air circulation around plants and pruning out and discarding infected portions.

Downy Mildew

One of the most commonly encountered fungal diseases in the garden, downy mildew—like most fungal disorders—is usually triggered by spells of wet, humid, or cool weather. Initially, yellow spots appear on the upper surface of leaves and the undersurface will have white, tan, or purplish downy mould. Eventually, leaves brown off as the tissue dies.

Susceptible plants: Grapes and many other ornamental and crop plants.

Controls: Seek out fungus-resistant varieties. Apply a preventive spray of Bordeaux mix or other copper-based fungicide that can also be used to halt the progress of the disease.

Powdery Mildew

Evidence of the disease's presence is a white, powderlike coating on foliage surfaces, resembling a light dusting with talc. Leaves develop spots or whitish patches and overall growth can become weak.

Susceptible plants: English Ivy, Euonymus, Grapes,

Powdery mildew and leafminer damage

Roses, and many other ornamentals.

Controls: There are many organic substances that either halt the spread of the disease or kill the spores. These include Bordeaux mix and other copper-based fungicides, sulfur, and lime-sulfur.

Rust Many rose species are susceptible to this debilitating disease that is evidenced by orangish or whitish blisters on leaves that often turn yellow and drop.

Susceptible plants: Roses and many other ornamentals.

Controls: Keep foliage dry by using drip irrigation or soaker hoses. Destroy diseased plant parts and use a sulfur dust or Bordeaux mix to contain spread.

BACTERIAL DISEASES

Fire Blight This disease is a serious threat to Cotoneasters, wilting, blackening, then killing new growth. If not checked, the entire plant may die.

Susceptible plants: Apple, Cotoneaster, Pyracantha, and many other ornamentals.

Controls: There is no cure, only control to keep it from spreading to healthy growth. Prune out and discard diseased tissue, taking out stems at least 6″ into green wood. Disinfect secateurs after each cut, as described earlier. The following spring, spray the shrub thoroughly with Bordeaux mix while it is in flower.

Leaf Spot Variously colored and shaped spots appear on leaves, especially during wet, humid periods, often spreading to cover the entire leaf. Eventually, infected leaves yellow and drop.

Susceptible plants: Boston Ivy, Virginia Creeper, and other ornamentals.

Controls: Prune out and destroy diseased portions of plants. Copper-based substances, such as Bordeaux mix, offer marginal control when used at one-week intervals. Preventive measures include not working around plants when their foliage is wet and disinfecting pruning tools after working on diseased plants.

Organic vs. Synthetic Pesticides

Throughout this book, controls recommended for eradicating or discouraging insect pests that damage vines and climbers are of organic origin and are environmentally responsible. Broad- and narrow-spectrum chemical pesticides work faster than organics but have grave consequences: They contaminate the environment, pose potential health risks to humans and animals, and kill beneficial insects along with pests.

Organics are often short-lived in their "kill potential," and repeat applications are sometimes necessary to produce effective results. The upside is that, if used responsibly, they pose no threat to beneficials, humans, or the environment. What is an organic substance? The word is being widely misused by some who recognize its profit potential. The classic and correct definition is anything that occurs naturally in nature, from *microbic, mineral, plant,* or *animal* sources. Anything synthesized or added to an organic substance (unless it, too, is organic) takes it out of the organic, or natural, category.

When organics are used, the fast knockdown of insects or the sustained control that chemical pesticides deliver isn't always obvious. As mentioned before, repeat treatments are often necessary since many organics have a brief life. Some lose their effectiveness quickly in sunlight. But in a world that is fast becoming overdosed with persistent and lethal chemical poisons, be willing to accept a small part of the responsibility we all share as caretakers of the Earth, and don't foul the nest for the coming generations. Seek organic solutions to problems in the garden.

Natural pest controls. Great strides have been made in the last decade in researching the usefulness of organic pesticides and insect predators in controlling the legions of destructive insects that damage and destroy ornamental and food crop plants. Today natural pesticides eradicate nearly every kind of plant parasite, and sources abound for obtaining beneficial insects to decimate innumerable plant damagers.

Following is a list of widely available natural pesticides and the pests they control. These are often packaged under a variety of trade names by the various companies that market them.

Bacillus thuringiensis is a microbal substance that is commonly sold as BTK. The toxins contained in BTK kill most of the larvae and caterpillars that feed on ornamental and food-crop plants. BTK interrupts the digestive process, paralyzing then killing pests that ingest it. Variants control beetles, weevils, and mosquitoes. BTK is available in dusts, granules, and liquids for spraying. Rated harmless to humans and other mammals. Follow label directions for application methods, timing, frequency of use, and precautions.

Effective against: Most caterpillars as well as coddling moth larvae.

Cautions: Pests may build up a resistance to BTK. Alternate with other controls.

Diatomaceous Earth DE is composed of the abrasive silica shells of algae called diatoms. When ingested, the sharp extensions of the shells pierce the insect's body, causing it to "bleed" to death internally. Available in dust form. Apply when foliage is wet for good adhesion. Can also be applied around the base of plants and watered in to control pests in the root zone.

Effective against: aphids, caterpillars, leafhoppers, thrips, slugs, snails, and many other soft-bodied pests.

Cautions: Although rated harmless to man and other mammals, inhalation of DE could cause irritation of mucous membranes. User should wear eye protection and a respirator. Harmful to some beneficial insects. Only natural-grade DE should be used.

Garlic Oil Spray One of the several home remedies that have proven somewhat useful in the garden, garlic juice mixed with pure soap and mineral oil as a spreader produces an effective insecticide for use against quite a few sap-sucking and leaf-chewing insects. Spray is prepared by chopping four cloves of garlic and stirring in a tablespoon of mineral oil. Steep the mixture overnight, then add two cups of water and stir in a teaspoon of unadulterated liquid dishwashing soap (not detergent). Mix thoroughly, then strain concentrate into a container. For use, dilute two tablespoons in one pint of lukewarm water and pour into a hand atomizer.

Effective against: Aphids, caterpillars, leafhoppers, mealybugs, and whiteflies. Marginally effective against some leaf-chewers.

Cautions: Harmful to most beneficials. Use when honeybees are inactive. Some plants may be injured by mixture. Test on a leaf and watch results before spraying entire plant.

Insecticidal Soap Made from fatty acids that are produced naturally by plants and animals, these easily biodegradable substances are effective against a number of soft-bodied sucking insects, but their control of chewing insects is spotty. They penetrate the insect's body, destroying membranes, and accumulate in their nervous system, leading to paralysis and death. Unlike many of the chemical pesticides, they break down quickly and leave no residual toxic material to contaminate the environment and pose no danger to humans and other mammals. Apply at the first sign of infestation and repeat weekly for a month, or until control is gained.

Effective against: Lethal to most soft-bodied pests—aphids, caterpillars, mealybugs, slugs, snails, and thrips.

Cautions: Since soaps also kill honeybees, spray early in the morning before they are active. Soaps may damage thin-leaved vines, so test first on one leaf and wait to see if a negative reaction occurs.

Neem A botanical extracted from seeds of the Malaysian margosa tree (*Azadirachta indica*). A naturally produced chemical in the seeds, azadirachtin, acts primarily as a feeding inhibitor.

Effective against: Aphids, leafminers, thrips, and whiteflies in their juvenile stage. There is no impact on adults.

Cautions: When applying, agitate to keep substance suspended in liquid.

Nicotine is a deadly alkaloid produced in varying degrees of potency by tobacco plants. It is available as a dust, or in concentrated liquid form (nicotine sulfate). Commercial nicotine sprays are available.

Effective against: Most sucking pests that feed on treated foliage.

Cautions: Toxic to humans and other mammals. Can be absorbed through the skin, eye tissue, and by breathing in sprays. Wear gloves, eye protection, and a respirator when mixing or spraying.

Oil Sprays (Dormant/Summer) Once, horticultural oils were only safe as dormant sprays (when plants were leafless), because heavy oil usually kills foliage. New oils are lighter, purer, and more versatile. They are sometimes referred to as summer, superior, or supreme oils, but they may retain their old trade name. They work by coating insects and their eggs with an impermeable layer of oil that smothers them. New-generation horticultural oils can be used as a dormant spray to control overwintering insects and as a summer spray to kill new invasions of pests.

Effective against: Most sucking and chewing insects, their larvae and eggs.

Cautions: Discuss proposed use with your nurseryman. Some plants may be harmed by oils. Follow label precautions and directions. Best used early in the morning.

Pyrethrin A botanical pesticide made from the dried flowers of *Chrysanthemum cinerariifolium.* It is often combined with other insecticides or fungicides for faster and more sustained control or for dealing with two problems at once. Pyrethrin is a nerve poison that is effective against a wide spectrum of chewing and sucking insects attacking ornamentals.

Effective against: Aphids, caterpillars, leafhoppers, mealybugs, mites, thrips, and whiteflies, and may provide some protection against other pests.

Cautions: Pyrethrins have been shown to kill ladybird beetles and are somewhat toxic to mammals. Hayfever sufferers may find using pyrethrins produces an allergic reaction. Follow label directions for use.

Rotenone A natural pesticide (often called derris) derived from tropical plants (derris, cube barbasco, and others). It is a stomach and contact poison and is often mixed with pyrethrin and ryania because of its potency. It is effective in protecting ornamentals against chewing insects, although its effectiveness is short-lived in hot, sunny weather. It is marginally effective against some sucking pests. Available as a dust, wettable powder, or concentrate.

Effective against: Caterpillars and Japanese beetles.

Cautions: Use the same precautions recommended for using nicotine substances.

Ryania is extracted from the shrub *Ryania speciosa.* It is a powerful botanical that knocks down a number of chewing and sucking pests. Can be used as a spray or dust.

Effective against: Aphids, coddling moths, Japanese beetles, and thrips.

Cautions: Use same protective measures as noted for mixing and applying nicotine. Don't use around ponds because of the toxic danger to aquatic life.

Sabadilla is another of the poisonous alkaloids that are effective against a wide range of garden pests. It is extracted from the seeds of the South American plant *Schoenocaulon officinale.* Begin spraying or dusting at the first sign of pests.

Effective against: Excellent kill rate against aphids,

caterpillars, grasshoppers, leafhoppers, stink bugs, and thrips.

Cautions: Not as toxic as nicotine-based extracts, but still should be handled responsibly. Lethal to honeybees, but harmless to other beneficials. Stores well in a dry, dark location.

Sticky Barriers

For years, gardeners have used non-toxic tacky substances made with castor oil, natural gum resins, and vegetable wax to block access to plants and trees to chewers and borers. Insects that try to pass through the barrier become trapped in the sticky goo. The best way to use sticky barriers on vines is to cut a 2″ wide piece of paper towel cardboard roller, slit it, and wrap it tightly around the stem(s) a few inches above the soil line. Secure the ends with masking tape. Then coat the bands with a ring of the substance.

Effective against: Ants, slugs, snails, and other crawling pests.

Cautions: Make certain all gaps are covered with sticky material. Replace weathered rings to maintain effectiveness. Remove during dormant period and replace in early spring.

10

Training, Pruning & Propagating Vines

Training and pruning could very easily be hyphenated, since they are intertwined. As one guides a vine up its support, pruning is often done at the same time to keep juvenile growth on the right path. The goal is to produce a vine that fits its space and develops the desired appearance and framework.

TRAINING VINES

Think of vines as malleable children. It is imperative that woody climbers be taken in hand in the early stages. Letting a vine behave as it wishes with the idea in mind of moderating its behavior sometime in the future is ill-advised. A vine that has been given free rein for a season or two develops a vigorous, wide-ranging root system and stems that are accustomed to going their own way. Trying to bring the vine under control after a long period of neglect is an almost hopeless undertaking. For each branch or entire stem that is removed, the overdeveloped root system will replace it with two or three. Eventually, one may be faced with uprooting the vine and starting fresh with a new one.

Often, when vines are purchased at the nursery, they are already trained on a stake driven into the container. This is done by the grower to keep the stems off the ground and from becoming a tangled mass of foliage. When the vine is transplanted, this stake should be removed. First of all, growers tend to lash the vine tightly against the stake with inflexible ties. If these are left in place, they will soon constrict the stems as they begin to expand, cutting into the bark and restricting the flow of sap. This could eventually stunt or kill the vine. Also, the stake interferes with the arrangement of stems in the proper manner on the vine's permanent support, for optimum growing and training.

There are two schools of thought on whether new plants should be pruned when they are set in. Historically, most vining plants (as well as broadleaf and bare root shrubs and trees) have been pruned to remove about a third of the growth on each branch or stem. This was thought to compensate for the loss of roots when bare roots and balled-and-burlapped plants (B&Bs) were dug and to promote branching and bushiness in broadleaf evergreens.

Current thinking among the experts is that this routine heading back is unnecessary and that evergreen plants need this additional leaf surface to gather energy.

There are pruning cuts that are undeniably beneficial to plants when they are first set in the garden: (1) to remove deadwood and broken branches; (2) to shape the vine and direct its growth; and (3) to encourage bushiness in vines that tend to become leggy (barren of foliage on the lower portion of their stems). Growing tips are snipped and long stems that have produced only sparse foliage along their length may be drastically headed back to let them start anew. It is a fact of botanical life that plants devote most of their growth energy to producing and sustaining new growth. When this tendency is frustrated by excising the stem tips, the plant responds by producing foliage from dormant nodes below the cut.

A grid of hardware cloth anchored to a wall provides an efficient trellis for climbers.

English Ivy may be quickly trained into a handsome espalier by installing a gridwork of wire.

Many vining plants, most climbers with weak tendrils, and all climbing roses need to be tied to their supports to train them in the desired growing pattern. Twiners and climbers require tying off only in their juvenile stage, before they have developed tendrils or begun to serpentine around their support. Other types that are not equipped to climb without guidance will need periodic tying off as they are directed up trellises, posts, and other vertical elements.

When training woody climbers, keep in mind that many species will bloom more profusely on branches that are trained horizontally. This is true of some other plant types, as well. Apples, for example, bear heaviest on branches that extend horizontally.

There are several types of ties that may be used to train vines. Most popular is the green plastic ribbon, available in varying widths (½″–1½″) and rolls from 25′–100′. It is soft and flexible yet durable and does not cut into stems. Additionally, because it is green it "disappears" among the foliage mass of the vine.

Also available in several widths and lengths are the flexible plastic "twist ties" that are reinforced with thin wire so they hold without tying when their ends are twisted together. These can cut into bark and soft stems, so they should never been twisted too tightly around canes or stems.

Another popular tying material is soft jute twine, which is quite strong and durable and, if not tied around stems too securely, will not constrict the wood.

The best way to use any tie is to make a loose figure-eight loop around the stem so it is loosely secured to the support. Ties should be checked periodically to ensure that they are not constricting growth and have not come loose under the weight of the vine.

Some gardeners make their own ties from strips cut from old nylon hose, cotton T-shirts and other flexible, non-binding material. These serve as well as the others, although their appearance may leave something to be desired.

For light- to medium-weight climbers that will be trained on walls and other vertical surfaces, a wide array of clamps and fasteners for this purpose are available at garden centers and through mail order sources. Most have a base that is affixed to brick,

Climbers without efficient holdfasts or tendrils often require anchoring with loosely tied twine or plastic gardener's ribbon.

stucco, or wood with adhesive and are equipped with twist ties or flexible wires for securing stems. These work well for the many annual and perennial vines that produce thin stems and modest foliage growth that won't put excessive stress on these light-duty fasteners.

PRUNING TIMING AND TECHNIQUES

Pruning of specific vining plants is described under that heading in the encyclopedia sections, but here are

Pruning *Actinidia* to one stem

Some vines need help to get started by weaving their stems through openings, such as here on a lattice trellis.

general guidelines to follow:

• Spring-flowering climbers are pruned when their blooming cycle ends, whatever the season. Pruning earlier would remove flowering wood. Heading back stems that have bloomed promotes the production of flowering wood for the next spring and summer.

• Summer- and fall-blooming types should be pruned in spring. Since these flower on the current season's wood, there is no loss of bloom.

• Deadwood and unproductive growth are taken out in both spring and fall, depending on the species and climate. Both are susceptible to disease and insect in-

vasions, which could threaten the entire plant.
• When pruning cuts are made, take the stem back to within ⅛″–¼″ of a node (or eye), or to the juncture of another branch. The goal is not to leave a stub, which will usually die back and sometimes take a viable stem with it.

Non-flowering broadleaf evergreens should be pruned in spring; needleleaf evergreens are rarely pruned (except to remove deadwood), since they do not recover their original form when stems are tipped back.

It bears repeating that pruning equipment must have sharply honed blades to avoid crushing plant tissue when cuts are made.

PROPAGATING CLIMBERS

Most vining plants may be increased without difficulty, provided the correct method is used for each species.

There are four basic methods of propagation—*seed, cuttings, division,* and *layers.* Some of these techniques were explained in the propagation entries of the encyclopedia sections.

Seed

Annual climbers and some perennials grown as annuals are almost always increased by seed. Even a few of the woody climbers may be seminally propagated, but these may not come true to species from collected seed. Also, growing these from seed means a long wait before plants of significant size are produced.

Most seeds of vining plants may be started indoors a few weeks before they can be safely planted or sown outdoors in spring in most sections of the country. These are germinated quite easily in a medium of vermiculite (or perlite) and milled peat moss that is kept evenly moist and placed in a warm, shaded location.

They transplant without incident, so they may be started in almost any container with good drainage.

Then there are those that require special treatment to spur germination. Some resent having their roots disturbed and do not transplant well when removed from their germination container. These include Balsam Apple, Cardinal Climber, Cathedral Bells, Cypress Vine, most gourds, and Moonflower. These seeds should either be sown in place or in peat pots that can be set in the garden without uprooting the plants from the container.

Peat pellets are excellent for starting seeds. On the left, the pellet has been soaked in water in preparation for seed-starting.

Peat is an organic substance and roots quickly grow through the porous sides and bottom of the pot. Eventually the peat decomposes, adding humus to the soil.

Seeds of other climbers have hard, moisture-impermeable coats and must either be scarified (nicked or filed) to break through the coating, or soaked overnight in hot (never boiling) water to soften the coat. Since nicking can sometimes injure a seed and destroy its viability, the safest method is soaking, which usually accomplishes the goal of breaking through the tough seed walls. Seeds of climbers that require this treatment include Cardinal Climber, Cypress Vine, most gourds, Moonflower, Morning Glory, and Chinese Wisteria.

Finally, a few seeds need to have their dormancy broken artificially to induce germination. In a natural setting these seeds are frozen by winter weather, then thawed by the arrival of spring's warming temperatures, which signal the seed enzymes to activate, and germination follows. This process may be simulated by sowing seeds in a moist medium composed of sand and milled peat moss, inserting the containers in plastic bags that are sealed and placed in the refrigerator or freezer a specified period.

Two climbing species that respond to this technique, called stratification, are *Campsis* and *Clematis*. Seeds of Trumpet Creeper are stored in the refrigerator for 8 weeks, then germinated at about 70°F. Clematis seeds are placed in the freezer for 3–4 weeks and germinated at about 80°F. Germination may not occur for several months.

Stem Cuttings

After seeds, rooting cuttings (vegetative propagation) is the most popular method of increasing one's stock. There are three types of cuttings. Most species can be propagated by employing one or more methods. These are *softwood*, *half-ripe*, and *hardwood* cuttings.

Select healthy, insect- and disease-free wood from which to strike cuttings. Use a sharp knife or single-edge razor blade to take softwood and half-ripe cuttings and use well-honed clippers to remove hardwood cuttings.

Softwood cuttings are taken in spring or summer. They should be young shoots of current season's wood. Ideally, the shoots are 2″–4″ long of growth originating from the crown of the plant. It isn't necessary to nip off the tip of the shoot, but any foliage that would be plunged under the surface when the cutting is inserted in the rooting medium should be pinched.

Stem cuttings usually require a few months to develop a root system capable of sustaining the propagated plant.

Half-ripe cuttings are struck in summer from wood produced on current season's growth and is halfway between softwood and hardwood in maturity. Sections should be 3″–4″ long. In both types, cuts should be made at the base of the shoot, just below a leaf joint or node, which is the source of the term "nodal cutting." As with softwood cuttings, strip the lower half of the cutting of its foliage.

Cuttings will root faster and more vigorously, in most cases, if their cut ends are lightly dusted with hormone rooting powder. Once the ends have been coated with rooting powder, tap the cuttings before inserting them in containers to remove excess powder, for only a light coating is necessary and too much interferes with the rooting process.

Hardwood cuttings are collected in late fall to early winter and are of ripened wood from the previous season's growth, or mature shoots from current season's wood. Length may range from 5″–8″. Cuts are made about ⅛″ above a bud, or eye, and just below a bud. The cut end, as before, is dipped in hormone rooting powder specifically formulated for hardwood cuttings. Make holes in the rooting compost with a pencil to receive the cuttings and plunge them halfway, firming the rooting mix around them.

Irrigate the newly set cuttings well and keep them just barely moist. Allowing the medium to dry out could result in the cuttings failing, especially after roots have begun to form. Fertilizer is not used in the process.

As indicated earlier, a good cutting medium is a mix of sharp sand, milled peat, and a small amount of vermiculite or perlite. Some gardeners prefer to use only sand for rooting cuttings, but sand dries out rapidly and requires continual monitoring to make certain the rooted cuttings are not deteriorating from dehydration.

Containers for rooting may be seed trays or small pots, either clay or plastic. Rooting is often hastened by inserting containers in polyethylene bags or covering them with a tent of polyethylene. Good results are

Kiwifruit cuttings are inserted in a rooting medium after having their cut ends dipped in a hardwood rooting hormone.

often obtained by setting cutting containers in a small, glass aquarium and covering the top with polyethylene or a sheet of glass. Several holes should be made in the polyethylene to evacuate excess moisture and thereby avoid mildew and other fungal diseases. The glass cover may be slid back half an inch to accomplish the same purpose. Whatever method is chosen, cuttings should be shaded and kept warm. Cuttings of some species root faster with bottom heat provided by horticultural heating cables. This is noted in the propagation notes of the encyclopedia sections.

Hardwood cuttings rooted outdoors need protection from the biting winds of winter and the effects of scorching of tender new growth in spring. A cold frame is an excellent rooting environment for most hardwood cuttings except those that need bottom heat to root. Among the latter are *Actinidia kolomikta, Celastrus,* and *Parthenocissus.* Some hardwood cuttings require several months to develop a root system that can sustain the plant. One should not be too eager to lift and transplant them.

Once rooting has occurred, cuttings should be potted up and held for a few months in a warm environ-

Cut ends of hardwood stem cuttings are dipped in rooting hormone; then the cuttings are inserted into prepared holes in the rooting medium.

ment (but without direct sunlight) while the root system expands. Once top growth is flourishing and the weather benign, begin the hardening-off process, setting cuttings outdoors in a shady nook during the day and bringing them in at night for a few weeks. If the weather is rainy, the cuttings will need protection from deluges that might wash them out of their container. Once they have been acclimated to the vagaries of outdoor temperatures and intense light, they may be set in the garden.

Leaf-Bud Cuttings

These are a form of softwood propagation. A number of climbers may be increased via this method, including *Clematis, Hedera,* and *Passiflora.*

With this method, one new-growth leaf, with a growth bud in the leaf axil and 1″–1½″ of its stem, is removed in early spring. Cut ends that will be plunged are dipped in hormone rooting powder. Stems are inserted in the rooting compost in prepared holes, the mix is firmed around them, and they are well watered. The methods for enhancing humidity and warmth around cuttings, described above, are recommended here also.

Eye Cuttings

Vitis sp. are commonly increased by this method. Sections of the vine, about 1½″ long, are taken from mature wood (previous season's growth) with an eye, or growth bud, at the top, about ⅛″ from the cut. The base cut is made between two buds, but the lower bud is removed. There are variations on this technique, but the above steps usually produce successful cuttings. As with most other cuttings, the base cut end is dipped in hormone rooting powder prepared for hardwood cuttings. A mix of sharp sand and milled peat is ideal for rooting eye cuttings. They are inserted ver-

Leaf cuttings whose cut ends have been dusted with a rooting hormone develop roots within a few weeks.

Leaf cuttings root faster if kept in a warm, moist environment. Here, a plastic bag with a few vent holes is used to create a greenhouse effect.

tically into the mix in small pots with only the dormant eye above the surface.

Divisions/Root Cuttings

A few herbaceous climbers may be propagated by division of their tubers and bulblets and others, such as *Anredera, Celastrus, Passiflora,* and *Wisteria,* may be started from sections of root cut into 6″ lengths and planted horizontally (vertically, if they are thick and fleshy) ½″ deep in the same rooting compost and using the same techniques recommended for cuttings. Take care that neither the cuttings nor the donor root dries out during the process. Keep the rooting medium barely moist throughout. Root cuttings will require a full season of growth to establish a vigorous root system.

Layers

There are three primary types of layers used in propagating climbers—*air layers, mound layers*, and *serpentine layers*. As one might expect from the term, the first is done aboveground, the others underground.

Air layers are made in spring and summer by making an angled cut about ¾″ long in a branch to create a tongue. A pebble or short piece of wooden matchstick is inserted under the tongue to keep it from closing and healing over. The cut is then dusted with hormone rooting powder and the area wrapped with moist sphagnum moss. Finally, the moss is enclosed in a piece of polyethylene and the ends are secured with twine or a twist tie. The moss should be examined periodically to ensure that it is moist, for if the moss dries out, the layer will more than likely fail.

Once roots have filled the moss, the layer is cut from the plant, immediately potted up in a fertile soil mix, and staked until the root system has developed sufficiently to support the cutting in an upright position.

Mound layers are created in the same season and in an almost identical manner. A supple, low-growing stem is selected and the same type of cut as for air layers is made. If the soil in which the donor plant is growing is not very fertile, a small area under the layer cut should be amended with compost containing a bit of vermiculite or perlite. The stem section containing the cut (without a cocoon of moss and polyethylene) is buried under a mound of the improved soil and either pegged in place with a notched stem or section of bent wire, or weighted down with a brick or stone. In 6–8 weeks, begin testing the layered section by tugging gently on it. Resistance means that roots have developed and layering was successful, but be advised that some woody climbers require eight months or longer to root.

When the layer has rooted sufficiently, if desired it may be dug up, severed from the branch (snip it off just below the root mass), and moved to another location or potted and held, if the weather has begun to turn cold, to wait for a more auspicious planting time.

Air layers are prepared by (1) making a 1″ long, angled cut in the stem, then (2) inserting a sliver of wood in the cut to prevent healing. (3) Finally, the cut section is wrapped in moist sphagnum peat moss, then plastic wrap.

Mound layers can be accomplished directly in containers, following the above steps.

Plants with long stems are appropriate for serpentine layers, which are made in spring and summer. Some species that are good candidates for this technique include *Hedera, Hydrangea petiolaris, Jasminum, Lonicera, Passiflora, Schizophragma, Vitis*, and *Wisteria*. New growth should be chosen for propagation. The technique is a variation on that which is used for mound layers. Diagonal cuts are made in the

Inserting the sliver of wood

Wrapping the cut section

stem about 2″ long in several places and the stem is also twisted at nodal points to fracture the bark and injure the tissue. The cuts are blocked open as before and prepared stem portions are buried in improved soil and pegged or weighted in place and kept evenly moist. Stem portions where rooting is desired may also be anchored in pots of prepared cutting compost. Adequate root systems capable of supporting the cuttings may require several months to develop. After this has transpired, rooted stems are lifted and sectioned to create transplants.

Once cuttings and layers brought along in a greenhouse or other interior location are flourishing and ready for transplanting in the garden (in the appropriate season), they need to be hardened off. This means slowly acclimating them to the extremes of temperature and to sun and wind. As touched on earlier, this is accomplished by moving them outdoors to a sheltered location during the day and returning them to their interior location before nightfall. This is done for several consecutive days or weeks. Even after the cuttings are planted outdoors, they should be watched for a while for signs of decline—wilting, flagging, scorching, or insect infestations on tender new growth.

PROPAGATION METHODS FOR VINES, VINE-LIKE PLANTS

Species	Seed	Softwood Cuttings	Half-Ripe Cuttings	Hardwood Cuttings	Layers	Root Cuttings	Divisions
Actinidia arguta, A. deliciosa		MS	M-LS	LF/EW			
Actinidia kolomikta	EF	EF	M-LS	LF/EW	MSP/ES		
Akebia quinata	EF		LS/EF		MSP/LS		
Ampelopsis sp.	EF	ES		LF/EW			
Anredera sp.						E-MW	
Aristolochia sp.	E-MSP		M-LS	LS	ESP/LS		
Asarina sp.	LW/ESP	EW					
Bryonopsis sp.	LW/ESP						ESP
Calonyction sp.	ESP		MS				
Campsis sp.	E-MSP		M-LS	ESP		E-LW	
Celastrus sp.	E-MSP	LF/EW		LF/EW	MSP/LS	E-MW	
Clematis sp.		MSP/ES[1]			MSP/LS		
Clerodendron sp.	MW/MSP	MSP/LS	MSP/LS				
Cobaea sp.	MW/MSP						
Cotoneaster sp.	E-MSP			LS/EF	MSP/LS		
Dioscorea sp.	EF	ESP/ES					
Dolichos sp.	ESP						
Eccremocarpus sp.	LW/ESP						
Euonymus fortunei			LS/EF		ES		
Fuchsia corymbiflora		S/F					
Gourds	ESP						
Hedera sp.		E-MS[1]			MSP/LS[3]		
Humulus sp.	MSP					E-MW	E-MSP
Hydrangea petiolaris	E-MSP			LF	MSP/LS[3]		
Ipomoea sp.	E-MS						
Jasminum sp.			M-LS	LF	MSP/LS[3]		
Lathyrus sp. Cl. Annual	E-MF						
Lathyrus sp. Cl. Perennial	E-MSP						E-MSP
Lonicera sp. Vining Climber			ES/LF		MSP/LS[3]		
Lonicera sp. Shrubby Climber	E-MSP						
Mandevilla sp.	E-MS		E-MS				
Maurandia sp.	ESP		MS				

Species	Seed	Softwood Cuttings	Half-Ripe Cuttings	Hardwood Cuttings	Layers	Root Cuttings	Divisions
Menispermum sp.	LW/ESP			LS/EF			
Momordica sp.	ESP						
Monstera sp.		E-LS	E-LS		SP/S		
Pandorea sp.	MW/MSP		M-LS				
Parthenocissus sp.	E-MSP	MSP/ES	LF/EW		MSP/LS		
Passiflora sp.	E-MSP	LSP/ES			MSP/LS[3]	E-MW	
Periploca sp.			M-LS		LS/EF		E-MSP
Phaseolus sp.	ESP						
Polygonum sp.	LW/ESP			M-LS			E-MSP
Pyrostegia sp.			LS				
Quamoclit sp.	ESP						
Rhoicissus sp.		E-LS[1]	E-LS				
Rosa sp. Ramblers				LF/EW			
Rosmarinus sp.			E-MF				
Schizandra sp.	E-MSP		LS		MSP/LS		
Solanum sp.			M-LS				
Stauntonia sp.			S				
Stephanotis sp.	MW/MSP		M-LS				
Thunbergia sp.		ES					
Trachelospermum sp.			LS		MSP/LS		
Tripterygium regelii	LW/ESP			LF/EW			
Tropaeolum sp. Annual	MSP						
Tropaeolum sp. Perennial	E-MSP	M-LS					
Tropaeolum peregrinum	LW/MSP						
Vitis sp.	E-MSP	E-MW[2]			MSP/LS[3]		
Wisteria sp.	E-MSP			LF/EW	MSP/LS[3]	E-MW	

KEY

SP = Spring
S = Summer
F = Fall
W = Winter

ESP = Early Spring
ES = Early Summer
EF = Early Fall
EW = Early Winter

MSP = Midspring
MS = Midsummer
MF = Mid-Fall
MW = Midwinter

LSP = Late Spring
LS = Late Summer
LF = Late Fall
LW = Late Winter

1 = Leaf-bud cuttings   2 = Eye cuttings   3 = Serpentine layers

GLOSSARY OF HORTICULTURAL TERMS

Acid, acidic   Having a pH value below 7.0.

Acuminate   Of leaves and bracts, ending with a tapered point, with concave sides.

Aerial (roots)   Roots emanating from an aboveground stem.

Alternate (leaves)   Solitary leaves developing at stem nodes, arranged singly at different heights and on different sides of the stem.

Annual   Lasting but one season.

Anther   Pollen-bearing portion of the stamen.

Apex   The tip or extreme end.

Attenuate   Describing leaf bases, gradually long-tapering to a point.

Axil   The upper angle between a leaf or branch and the stem on which it is carried.

Backfill (soil)   Soil removed from a planting hole or bed.

Boss   A raised protuberance in the center of a flower usually containing the sexual parts.

Bract   A modified leaf or leaflike scale, often encasing the true flower.

Bud eye, eye   A dormant bud in the axil of a leaf, stem.

Bud union   The section of a grafted plant that is between the understock and the variety grafted onto it.

Calyx   Collectively, the sepals of a flower.

Compound   Comprising two or more similar parts.

Cordate   Heart-shaped or ovate.

Corolla   Collectively, the petals of a flower.

Corona   The portion of a flower extending between the corolla and the stamen.

Crown   The point where the lower trunk meets the rootstock.

Cultivar   A variety bred or propagated by man as opposed to a naturally occurring form.

Cupped form (flowers)   In describing rose blossoms, having an open center revealing the stamens.

Cutting   Any vegetative part of a plant taken for propagation.

Deltoid   Triangular, or shaped in the form of the Greek letter delta.

Dentate   Having sharp, spreading teeth.

Dioecious   Bearing unisexual (separate sex) flowers on separate plants.

Dormant   Living, but not growing. The resting stage.

Elliptic, elliptical   Oblong, narrowed at the ends and widest in the center.

Entire   Not dentate. Undivided. With a smooth, continuous margin.

Filament   A threadlike organ, commonly the anther-bearing stalk in a stamen.

Floriferous   Bearing flowers.

Funnelform   With a funnel, or tube, gradually expanding towards the mouth.

Glabrous   Smooth and hairless.

Habit   The growth pattern and appearance of a plant.

Hastate   Shaped like an arrowhead with basal lobe turned outward.

Heel cutting   A short cutting containing a portion of the older stem.

Herbaceous   Soft-tissued. Not woody.

High-centered   Usually used in describing hybrid tea rose blooms. A bloom whose central petals are longer than those surrounding them.

Hirsute   With coarse, stiff hairs.

Hispid   With prickly, stiff hairs.

Keel   A ridge, as on a leaf.

Lanceolate   Shaped like a lance. Pointed at the apex, longer than broad, with broadest portion below the center.

Lateral   Emanating from the side.

Layer, layering   In propagation, sections of branches and stems that are wounded to induce the formation of roots.

Leaflet   A unit of a compound leaf.

Lobe   Describing leaves, a portion separated from another by an indentation that usually extends only halfway.

Microclimate   An area within another (such as a valley between two hills) that has a much different climate from the area that surrounds it.

Monoecious   Containing unisexual (separate sex) flowers on the same plant.

Mouth   The broadest point on the tube opening of a funnelform flower.

Node   The juncture on a stem where one or more leaves emanate.

Obovate   A leaf that is longer than it is broad and rounded at the ends.

Organic   Anything that is produced naturally in nature. Not man-made.

Ovate   Egg-shaped. Often used to describe the widest part of a leaf near the leaf stalk, but also used to describe leaves rounded at both ends and widest in the center.

Panicle   In describing flowers, a loosely branched cluster of blossoms.

Pendant, pendent   Dropping downwards.

Peduncle   The stalk of a solitary flower or cluster of flowers.

Perennial   A plant of more than two seasons' duration.

Petiole   The stalk of a leaf.

Pinnately compound   A compound leaf whose leaflets are arranged on both sides of a common axis. Featherlike.

Pistil   The female organ of a flower, made up of a stigma, a style below the stigma, and, below this, an ovary which evolves into the seed capsule.

Racemes   The unbranched flower cluster with a primary stalk from which individual flowers emerge.

Root-hardy   Roots that survive freezing temperatures.

Salverform   Of flowers, having a slender tube and abruptly expanding petals.

Scarify   To injure the seed case by abrading or cutting to hasten germination.

Seminal (propagation)   Propagating with seed.

Sepal   A modified leaf that forms part of a flower.

Single   Of flowers: with 5–12 petals. Of varieties: one bloom per stem.

Spathe   Bract which encloses a flower cluster or spadix (floral spike).

Sport   Different from the normal. A mutation that occurs naturally.

Stamen   The male organ of a flower that includes a pollen-bearing anther or an anther and filament.

Stigma   The terminal portion of a pistil that receives pollen and spurs germination.

Stolon   A runner or stem that spreads over the surface of the soil.

Tendril   A thin, coiling extension by which plants cling to supports and climb.

Terminal   The end of a stem or branch.

Tomentose   Densely covered with short hairs.

Vegetative   In propagation, the use of a part of a plant's tissue for increasing stock, as opposed to seminal, or seed, propagation.

INDEX

Page numbers in *italics* indicate artwork; those in **boldface** indicate both text and artwork.

INDEX

GLEN COVE PUBLIC LIBRARY

3 1571 00155 1186

635.974   Crandall, Chuck.
C

Flowering, fruiting &
foliage vines.

DATE			

GLEN COVE PUBLIC LIBRARY
GLEN COVE, NEW YORK 11542
PHONE: 676-2130
DO NOT REMOVE CARD FROM POCKET

BAKER & TAYLOR